D0443961

You are not alone...

1,000 *

unforgettable

SENIOR MOMENTS

by TOM . . . uh . . . FRIEDMAN

{ *OF WHICH WE COULD REMEMBER ONLY 246* }

WORKMAN PUBLISHING • NEW YORK

Library of Congress Cataloging-in-Publication Data is available.

ISBN-13: 978-0-7611-4076-4

Workman books are available at special discounts when purchased in bulk for premiums and sales promotions as well as for fund-raising or educational use. Special editions of book excerpts can also be created to specification. For details, contact the Special Sales Director at the address below.

Design by Paul Hanson

Workman Publishing Company, Inc.
225 Varick Street
New York, NY 10014-4381
www.workman.com

Printed in Mexico

First printing April 2006

10 9 8

To Christy, Corey, and Jonathan

INTRODUCTION

Wouldn't it be great if there were some way to alleviate the confusion and isolation of suffering senior moments? Wouldn't it be great if there were a book of classic senior moments experienced throughout history by some of the most illustrious men and women who ever lived, to remind you that not only is there life after senior moments, but also great art to be created, Nobel Prizes to be won, possibly even the reason for going into the next room to be remembered?

By sheer chance, you're holding such a book in your hands—*1,000 Unforgettable Senior Moments.* It's an indispensable volume for all of you who are unable to conjure up either the first or last name of the person who just came up to you and said, "It's so good to see you again!" It's the book you will want to carry with you at all times so that you can open it at any page and see that Albert Einstein, Ralph Waldo Emerson, Jimmy Carter, and countless others have experienced major mental lapses that make your own . . . well, hardly worth remembering.

If you're middle-aged, as I am, the first thing you may want to know about senior moments is: Are they really senior? I'm often asked this, and although I can't recall what I've said, I do have my notes, which suggest that the answer is yes, no, and maybe.

The most familiar type of forgetting is absentmindedness, in which information is never properly encoded in one's memory, if it's encoded at all. Say you've misplaced your keys. When you laid them down, you weren't giving their location your full attention, you were distracted, or, as scientists say, your attention was "divided."

But these memory lapses can be junior moments as well as senior ones. After all, teenagers who are walking almanacs of useless information can lose one jacket after another, making their parents crazy. They can study all night for a test and in the morning forget everything they learned if the information isn't encoded in their memories.

But it *is* true that as we get older, we do seem to suffer senior moments more often. Certainly, we're more conscious of our forgetfulness as we age, whereas kids tend to shrug it off. The stakes are higher for us. We have more things to do, more responsibilities.

But even that's not the whole story. If we learn a new, less-than-earth-shaking piece of information (say, that the average Emperor penguin weighs 66 pounds and eats squid, fish, and krill), but we don't have a reason to use it soon after, imprinting it in our memory, it may never stick. It's not that there isn't enough "room" in our memory to fit everything in; it's just that, as we grow older, we tend to remember the more important stuff and don't bother as much as we used to with information about Emperor penguins. That's why I like to think of senior moments as evidence of having a more discriminating mind. (You might want to use this line yourself the next time your loved ones get exasperated with you.)

Forgetting even serves an important function for our species. What would our lives be like if we didn't forget anything— if we remembered every bad movie we ever sat through, every face we saw, every argument we had? How could we function if our attention couldn't be divided? Driving, eating, having sex, and following the plots of political thrillers, to name just a few things, would be impossible. What are a few intensely irritating memory lapses compared to the nightmare of remembering *everything*?

There are also enormous differences among individuals in their ability to remember, no matter what their age. A seventy year old can have a better memory than an eighteen year old. (When my grandmother was ninety-four, she could remember every student she taught in a Hungarian high school, while I couldn't remember where I parked my car. West 88th Street? Budapest?)

That's the good news. (You may want to stop reading now and go directly to the contents of this book.) For those of you who are not only forgetful but masochistic, here's the bad news: There's another type of forgetting—called "transience"—that does occur with the passage of time. A number of studies have shown that seniors in general have more difficulty remembering information they've been asked to learn than college students do. Even when older people recall information as well as younger folk do, their memories fade faster. They have more trouble remembering the precise details of something, even when they can still recall the gist of it.

There's another variant of forgetting that can be age related, as well. It occurs when something has been stored in your memory, but you can't retrieve it when you need to. For some, this is the most diabolical senior moment of all. It's the information that's on the "tip of your tongue." Scientists, who are an unpoetic lot, call it "blocking."

Blocking happens more often among older people than younger people, more often among forty year olds than twenty year olds, more often among seventy year olds than forty year olds. These senior moments really *are* senior. Proper names are easiest to block because often they're not accompanied by context clues; they're not very well integrated with related concepts, knowledge, and associations that might jog your memory. The odds of recalling the proper name Burns would be far greater, for instance, if it referred to an ER doctor, but that would be too easy, wouldn't it?

Now, there are a lot of books you can buy and courses you can take about how to add context clues to names and other bits of information, and there are sales people and politicians who seem born with the ability to remember names and places, just as there are absentminded people who seem destined to wander the earth incapable of remembering where they're going and where they've come from. But if you're not going to devote enough time, energy, and money to improving your memory significantly as you get older, I would recommend my approach, which is easier and cheaper. Just mumble, "It's so nice to see you," when cornered by someone whose name you can't recall, and avoid at all costs playing Trivial Pursuit, chess, and poker.

Look at it this way: If you can't recall who your spouse is, you have a big problem and need professional help right away. Otherwise, you might as well laugh it off, which is what I try to do. When I can remember.

This book will definitely help you laugh it off. And here's the best part: You can read it over and over again and it will seem as fresh and funny as the day you bought it! Feel free to misplace it, so you can buy another copy—and another, and another, over and over again!

Embrace your senior moments! Just don't try to remember them.

—T. F.

SU CASA ES MI CASA

Columbia University philosopher Irwin Edman once visited the home of a colleague. At 2 A.M. Edman's colleague began to yawn pointedly. When Edman didn't take the hint, the man said, "Irwin, I hate to put you out, but I have a nine o'clock class tomorrow morning." "Good Lord!" Irwin replied, "I thought you were in *my* house!"

WAIT, I CHANGED MY MIND— MAKE THAT GRUEL

The Marquis de Condonset had what seemed to be a good idea for escaping the Reign of Terror during the French Revolution. He dressed up as a peasant in ragged clothes and took off. Just before he reached the French border, he stopped at an inn full of hungry locals and, completely forgetting his disguise, ordered an extravagant omelet made with a dozen eggs. Instead of a meal, he got the guillotine.

THE FIRST ANNUAL G. K. CHESTERTON AWARD FOR ABSENTMINDEDNESS GOES TO . . . G. K. CHESTERTON!

The notoriously absentminded and disorganized British writer G. K. Chesterton was devoted to his mother. When he became engaged, he shared the happy news by writing a long letter to her. It would have been an even more thoughtful gesture had his mother not already been sitting in the same room when he wrote it.

BETTER YET, HAVE HIM CALL ME

One evening the German dramatist and philosopher Gotthold Ephraim Lessing, who was lost in thought, realized he had forgotten his house key. When he knocked on his front door, a servant looked out the window and, not recognizing Lessing in the dark, called out, "The professor is not at home," to which the notoriously absentminded Lessing replied, "Oh, very well. No matter." He then turned around and started walking away, saying: "Tell him I'll call another time."

BEATS "HEY, YOU"

Because he couldn't remember anyone's name, Chuck Berry called everyone Jack. Zsa Zsa Gabor, who was once asked about her equally bad memory, replied, "Dahling, how do you think the 'dahling' thing got started?"

BUT HE DID REMEMBER
IT WAS LONDON

In October 1944 Welsh poet Dylan Thomas failed to appear at his friend Vernon Watkins's London wedding, where Thomas was scheduled to serve as best man. After the ceremony, Watkins received an envelope from Thomas. It contained two letters. The first one apologized for having forgotten the name of the church. The second apologized for having forgotten to mail the first letter.

ALTHOUGH NOT AS GREAT
AS IT COULD HAVE BEEN

When Richard Nixon arrived in Paris for the funeral of French President Georges Pompidou in April 1974, his mind must have been elsewhere. At the airport he declared, "This is a great day for France!"

AND PLEASE GIVE MY REGARDS
TO HIS LOVELY WIFE

Sir Thomas Beecham (1879–1961), the founder of the London Philharmonic Orchestra, once ran into a distinguished-looking woman in the lobby of a hotel. Although he could not remember her name, he thought he knew her. When he engaged her in conversation, he vaguely recollected that she had a brother. Hoping for any clue to her identity, he asked her how her brother was and whether he was still working at the same job. "Oh, he's very well," said Princess Mary about George VI, "and still king."

AND IT'S ENTIRELY POSSIBLE
I HAD PARENTS, TOO

Drew Barrymore was asked by *Premiere* magazine in 2001 whether she hoped to have children. "Definitely!" she said. "I would like to have at least two, because I didn't have a brother or sister growing up." Suddenly she paused. "I mean, I *have* a brother, but we didn't really spend a lot of time together." Again, she stopped. "And I have a sister too!"

THAT'S OKAY, HE WOULDN'T HAVE
FOUND A RAZOR ANYWAY

A friend of Ludwig van Beethoven's named Frederick Stark called on him one morning and found the great but forgetful composer in his bedroom, getting dressed. Curiously, Beethoven's face was covered with a thick layer of dried soap. He had lathered his face the night before, planning to shave, then forgot to do so and went to bed.

OH, I THOUGHT MOZART
GOT IT FROM ME

Once, while in London, singer-songwriter Neil Diamond heard some familiar music and mentioned that it was from his hit "Song Sung Blue." His companion quickly corrected him, saying, "No, they're playing Mozart." "Oh," said Diamond, who had conveniently forgotten he borrowed the music from Mozart's Piano Concerto No. 21.

THAT'S ONE SMALL MISSTEP
FOR MAN . . .

In 1969 astronaut Neil Armstrong prepared and rehearsed the single line he was going to say when he became the first man to step on the moon. He was supposed to say, "That's one small step for *a* man, one giant leap for mankind." Instead he said, "That's one small step for man, one giant leap for mankind"—which made no sense, since *man* and *mankind* are synonymous. No matter—the history books reinstated the "a." Unfortunately, the famous line is almost always spoken incorrectly—just the way Armstrong said it.

LET'S HAVE HIM OVER FOR DINNER AS SOON AS POSSIBLE

The names of friends and acquaintances often escaped the mind of playwright Howard Lindsay (1889–1961). Sometimes this had unexpected consequences, as when he was engaged in a long, bitter feud with a particular actor. For years he refused to stay in the same room with him when they accidentally met, but one evening Lindsay's wife was astonished to find her husband engaged in a warm conversation with his nemesis at a Hollywood dinner party. The conversation ended with a burst of laughter, and after Lindsay slapped the actor on the back, he came over to his wife and whispered in her ear, "Who was that fellow I was just talking to, anyhow?"

WHERE WAS THE INVISIBLE HAND
WHEN HE NEEDED IT?

Adam Smith, the founding father of modern economics and the author of *The Wealth of Nations,* was notoriously absentminded. He once put bread and butter into a teapot and, after tasting the result, declared it to be the worst cup of tea he had ever had.

JUST DON'T SIT TOO CLOSE
TO THE HEAD

In 1991 members of the Georgia State Game Commission were going back and forth, considering the merits of an item on their agenda: the regulation of alligator rides. There were some testy exchanges before one alert official—obviously the only alert one in the room—realized that, thanks to an assistant's typo, they were discussing a nonexistent recreation instead of the real agenda item: a discussion of regulating the sale of alligator *hides.*

NEXT YEAR LET'S ASSIGN HIM TO THE POLE VAULT

It was the 1932 Olympics, and competitors in the 3,000-meter race were coming around the bend for the final lap. Unfortunately, an official was gazing in the wrong direction and therefore neglected to ring the bell to signal the last lap. After the athletes crossed what should have been the finish line, they just kept on running. The favorite to win, a Finn named Volmari Iso-Hollo, wound up first, but because he ran an extra 450 meters before the official snapped out of his senior moment, he registered the slowest-ever time for the 3,000.

WE WANTED THAT FRESH, OPEN LOOK

A new jail in Jacksonville, Duval County, Florida, was about to open in 1995. It cost $35 million to build and was everything a community could want in a prison—except for one minor problem: County officials forgot to order doors for the 195 cells.

THIS SURE IS ONE SATISFYING
BILDUNGSROMAN

The Russian critic and philosopher Mikhail Bakhtin was working on a major new work on the "bildungsroman," a novel of spiritual, moral, or psychological development. Working furiously to finish it, Bakhtin, a heavy smoker, suddenly found himself without any rolling paper to make cigarettes, an intolerable situation. Not having money to spare, he absentmindedly looked around his room for a substitute and grabbed the first thing at hand, thus managing, over the next couple of hours, to smoke away an important section of his manuscript.

NO, NO, NOT THE OTTOMAN!

For a scene she was shooting for 1959's *Some Like It Hot*, Marilyn Monroe was supposed to enter a room, walk to a dresser, rummage through the drawers, find a bottle of bourbon, and ask for a drink. She blew the line 52 times in a row—although far

from her record of 82 takes, set earlier
by the famously forgetful movie star.
"On the fifty-third take," recalled director
Billy Wilder, "I told her we had put the
line on pieces of paper, and they were in
every drawer she would open." However,
added Wilder, "she went to the wrong
piece of furniture."

I'LL TAKE THE FORTIES, TOO,
IF YOU GOT 'EM

An out-of-work shoe salesman, who
was trying to make ends meet, decided
to rob a bank in Queens, New York. The
beginning of the note he handed to the
teller demonstrated a keen recall of U.S.
currency denominations: "Give me all your
tens, twenties . . . ," it began. But then his
memory failed him: ". . . and thirties," the
note concluded.

AND THE ONE ABOUT "FOUR SCORE AND SEVEN YEARS AGO"—THAT WAS MINE, TOO

Sometimes *pretending* you had a senior moment saves the day. Raconteur and Republican senator from New York Chauncey M. Depew was chosen to speak after Mark Twain at a banquet. As Depew watched, Twain delivered an uproarious talk. Depew walked to the dais, waited until the laughter and applause had died down, and then cannily feigned forgetfulness. "Mr. Toastmaster and Ladies and Gentlemen," he announced, "before this dinner Mark Twain and myself agreed to trade speeches. He has just delivered my speech, and I am gratified for the pleasant way in which you received it. I regret to say that I have lost the notes of *his* speech and cannot remember anything he was to say. Thank you."

"HOPE YOU LIKE IT!"

English clergyman and writer William Lisle Bowles once gave a parishioner a Bible as a birthday present. When she asked him to write an inscription, he signed it "From the Author."

DOES THAT MEAN I DON'T HAVE YOUR VOTE?

Tennessee senator Howard Baker was once walking from the Senate floor to his office when a group of tourists stopped him. One man said, "Say, I know who you are. Don't tell me. Let me remember. I'll get it in a minute." Baker waited patiently for the man's memory to return. Finally the senator said, "Howard Baker." The tourist shook his head, still in the grip of his senior moment: "No, that's not it."

OFF COURSE

When race car driver Buddy Baker blew out a tire and slammed into a wall during a race in Tennessee, he suffered a minor concussion and broken ribs. He was then strapped to a rolling stretcher and loaded into an ambulance, but the ambulance driver forgot to shut the rear door tightly. When the ambulance lurched forward, Baker, stretcher and all, rolled onto the track—where, much to Baker's horror, the other cars were heading straight for him. Luckily, a warning flag cautioning the drivers to slow down was raised as soon as the accident occurred, but, of course, even a slower-moving race car can kill you. The medics ran after the stretcher, pushed it off the track, and were about to roll Baker back into the ambulance when he insisted on being strapped into the front seat instead, figuring that at least there he couldn't roll out the back door. But on the way to the hospital, the ambulance driver forgot to stop for a red light, narrowly missed an oncoming car, drove up onto the sidewalk, and smashed into a bunch of garbage cans. After Baker was treated by a doctor, the medics asked him if he'd like to be taken back to the track. He declined.

FURTHERMORE, WE SHALL FIGHT THEM ON THE BEACHES

The Baroness Trumpington of Sandwich stood up and began addressing the House of Lords about the wages paid to babysitters and nannies. "There has been much confusion on this matter," she declared, more accurately than she knew. After five minutes of an increasingly heated speech, she suddenly stopped and said, "My lords, I have been speaking on the wrong subject." Members of the House had been debating an amendment to a social security bill when the baroness took the floor and began reading from the wrong notes.

U2, BONO?

Bono (born Paul Hewson) of the rock group U2 often loses things, from keys and money to socks and underwear. But those are the minor senior moments. In 1981, before recording the album *October,* he couldn't find the lyrics to the songs anywhere and was forced to write new ones in the studio. The original lyrics were returned 24 years later, after they mysteriously turned up in a woman's attic.

YOU CAN'T IMAGINE HOW HARD IT WAS TO FIND PARTS

Robert Challender of Reno, Nevada, forgot to register his 1978 Datsun until a month after the deadline. The Nevada Department of Motor Vehicles, experiencing an institutional senior moment, sent him a late-fee bill of $378,426, of which $260,000 was for penalties dating back to 1900, when there were no automobiles in Nevada, let alone Japanese imports.

WHOSE NAMES ARE ON
THE TIP OF HIS TONGUE

In 1990 former *Partridge Family* star Danny Bonaduce met his wife, Gretchen, on a blind date. He married her that same day. According to the actor, when he woke up beside his new bride the next morning, he had to ask her for her name. In spite of this inauspicious start, they're still together and have two children.

AND, WHILE YOU'RE AT IT, DO YOU
MIND LOOKING AT MY TOAST-R-OVEN?

During a 1996 meeting of county commissioners, the controller in Reading, Pennsylvania, complained that her computer hadn't worked in two years, and that during the entire time she had been forced to use a typewriter for all her letters and memos. She probably would have had grounds for some legal action had it not been for the discovery soon after that she had forgotten to plug her computer in.

NEXT TIME I'LL WEAR A COAT WITH A ZIPPER

Essayist Charles Lamb encountered Samuel Coleridge one day on Hampstead Heath, in London. Coleridge took hold of one of the buttons on Lamb's coat, pulled him aside, and began to expound on a subject that was on his mind. A short time later, Lamb remembered that he was due elsewhere. Seeing no other means of escape, he took out his pocketknife and cut off the button that Coleridge was still clutching, leaving it in the poet's hand. Some hours later, Lamb returned to find Coleridge in the same spot, talking to himself on the same subject. Lamb then took up his former position while Coleridge, with the button still in his hand, continued to hold forth, apparently not having noticed his friend's absence.

I REALLY MUST START
EATING LESS OPIUM

Thomas De Quincey, the author of *The Confessions of an English Opium Eater*, was so absentminded that he often had trouble with the most straightforward tasks. He needed help dressing himself, and while looking over manuscripts by candlelight, he sometimes forgot what he was doing and set fire to his hair. A prodigious collector of books, he would fill his apartment with them until every last nook and cranny was filled, at which point he would resort to an ingenious solution: He would abandon the entire collection and move to another apartment.

B=SECOND SHELF FROM TOP[2]

Photographer Ernst Haas took a famous picture of Albert Einstein, which shows the great physicist thoughtfully rubbing his chin, as if he were pondering the mysteries of the universe. In fact, the picture was taken right after Haas asked Einstein where on the shelf he had put a particular book.

THE PONY EXPRESS IS LOOKING BETTER AND BETTER ALL THE TIME

The world's first airmail flight was scheduled to take off from Washington D.C.'s Potomac Park at 11:30 A.M. on May 14, 1918. You could feel the excitement: A large, expectant crowd had gathered, and even President Wilson was on hand. But the engine of the Curtis Jenny airplane just wouldn't start. A squad of mechanics checked everything they could think of, but thirty minutes passed without success. The president was far from pleased—and he was even less pleased when a mechanic finally thought to check the fuel tank, which was empty.

YOU MEAN WE'RE GOING TO A *REAL* JAIL?

A man attempting to rob a Bank of America branch in Merced, California, didn't have a gun, so he tried what he thought was the next best thing: He hid his finger in his jacket pocket and pointed it at the teller. The man then experienced an incredible senior moment: He took his finger out of his pocket and pointed it at the teller, demanding money. He even cocked his thumb. The teller, trying not to laugh, told him to wait and called the police, who arrested him—using real handcuffs.

INCIDENTALLY, WHO'S THE PIANIST THIS EVENING?

One evening at a concert, the Polish-born pianist Josef Casimir Hofmann (1876–1957) sat down at his piano with a look of confusion. The other members of the orchestra waited, becoming increasingly alarmed. Finally, Hofmann leaned toward a woman in the first row of the audience and whispered, "May I please see your program, madam? I forget what comes first."

NEXT WEEK WE'LL BE HONORING
SERGEANT WOOLWORTHS

Britain's greatest World War II general, Field Marshal Bernard Law Montgomery, attended a 1946 dinner given in his honor in Hollywood by MGM's Samuel Goldwyn. Famous for his senior moments, Goldwyn began his introduction ably: "It gives me great pleasure tonight to welcome to Hollywood a very distinguished soldier." He then raised his glass and said to the gathering of celebrities, "Ladies and gentlemen, I propose a toast to . . . Marshall Field Montgomery." There was a stunned silence, since Marshall Field was and is a famous department store in Chicago. Into the breech came another mogul with a bad memory, Jack Warner of Warner Brothers, who called out helpfully, "Montgomery Ward, you mean."

ROYALLY SCREWED UP

Sometimes a senior moment that should have led to an utter debacle is neatly handled by quick thinking and hard-earned experience. Lawrence Barrett, a great 19th-century actor and theater manager, was forced to hire an elderly friend at the last minute to replace someone in the important role of the king. The friend's role was to shout out orders to Barrett, but when the time came for the old actor to begin, the senior citizen experienced a very senior moment. At a loss, he ad-libbed to Barrett, "Come here!" Expecting the worst, Barrett walked over to the throne. His friend whispered into his ear that he couldn't remember a single line. At a complete loss, Barrett bowed and headed off stage. But just as Barrett approached the wings, he heard a royal-sounding command from his old friend: "Forget nothing I have told you!" The audience never suspected that anything was wrong.

AT LEAST IT WAS BACK
FROM THE LAUNDRY

Hans Hotter, the bass baritone who in 1937 began playing his most famous role, Wotan, the German god, in Wagner's opera *Die Valküre*, was getting ready to make his grand entrance in Act III one evening. He absentmindedly grabbed his cloak from his dressing room, flung it around his shoulders, and strode onto the stage, whereupon the audience began to snicker. Sticking out of the back of the cloak was the coat hanger it had been hanging on. Worse, the hanger was a padded pink one.

STRIKE THAT LAST REMARK
FROM THE RECORD

In 2004 Australian judge Dean Mildren declared he was "absolutely staggered" that a notorious burglar had been freed on bail for the third time in a year, even after flagrantly ignoring a court-imposed curfew. Mildren demanded to know the identity of the idiot jurist. He was quietly reminded that he was the idiot.

THE SECOND ANNUAL G. K. CHESTERTON AWARD FOR ABSENTMINDEDNESS GOES TO . . . G. K. CHESTERTON!

One day British writer G. K. Chesterton was hurrying down the street, late for a critically important appointment. But first, finding himself thirsty, he stopped off for some refreshment, a glass of milk at the local dairy that he had visited as a child. Next he bought a revolver at a gunsmith's shop, which he had been meaning to do for some time. Only then did he manage to remember where he was supposed to be going—his own wedding.

WAIT TIL YOU SEE WHAT
I'M GETTING FOR YOU *NEXT* WEEK

When he was the Democratic Senate majority leader, Lyndon Johnson ran into New Hampshire Republican Norris Cotton in the Senate elevator. "Norris," cried LBJ, "I've been looking for you. Come into my office." Johnson took a small box from his desk and presented it to Cotton with great fanfare. "Norris, when I was in Mexico recently, I had some cuff links made to give to a few personal friends in the Senate, and this is the first opportunity I have had to present them to you." Cotton told Johnson he was touched and would always cherish them. About three weeks later, Cotton bumped into LBJ again. Johnson grabbed him and cried, "Norris, I've been looking for you. Come into my office." For the second time, Johnson presented him with a small box. It was another pair of cuff links. "Norris," he said, "when I was in Mexico recently, I had some cuff links made to give to a few personal friends in the Senate . . ."

AND THE GUY STANDING
NEXT TO YOU IS MARC ANTONY

Twentieth Century–Fox Studios chief Spyros Skouros had a terrible memory for names. One day on the set of *Cleopatra,* a female cast member came up to him and said, "You don't know my name, do you?" "Yes, I do," he answered. The beautiful actress taunted him. "You're paying me $1 million and you can't remember my name! Spyros, tell me my name! I'll give you half the money back!" said Elizabeth Taylor. Skouros struggled to remember. "Ehh . . . ehh . . . you are Cleopatra!"

LET'S SEE, THAT WOULD MAKE IT
FOUR-THIRTY IN JERUSALEM

In Cecil B. DeMille's 1935 film *The Crusades,* Henry Wilcoxen, who played King Richard the Lionheart, forgot what century he was in. When he tossed back his cloak, the audience got a good look at his wristwatch.

YOU SHOULD SEE ME BEHIND
THE WHEEL OF A JEEP

When General George Metaxas, the dictator of Greece, was inspecting one of his air bases in the 1930s, he was invited to pilot a seaplane. Pleased, Metaxas took it up for a spin. But when the base commander, who accompanied the general, realized Metaxas was about to land on the runway, he diplomatically suggested that it might be better to land on the water, given that they were in a flying boat. Metaxas apologized for his absentmindedness and made a safe landing. When he arose from the captain's seat, he thanked the commander for his tact, opened the door, and promptly fell into the sea.

NOW IF I CAN ONLY REMEMBER WHERE
I PUT THAT TEST TUBE OF PLAGUE

In what may be one of the scariest senior moments in history, a nuclear bomb was discovered at the bottom of a deep mine shaft at a test site in Kazakhstan. It had been put there in 1991, ready to be set off, if necessary, as part of a Soviet testing program. But then the Soviet Union collapsed, Kazakhstan became independent, with no need of nuclear weapons, and the bomb was completely forgotten.

TAKE THAT,
YOU ABSENTMINDED GENIUS!

A rchimedes, today counted as one of the greatest figures in the history of science and mathematics, was recognized as a giant in his own time as well. So when the Romans stormed the Greek city of Syracuse, where Archimedes was living, a Roman soldier was given orders to bring him before the admiring emperor. But when the soldier repeatedly tapped the absentminded mathematician on the shoulder to get his attention, Archimedes was so absorbed in a problem he had traced in the dust, he did not react. Infuriated by the "insult," the soldier drew his sword and killed him.

I'D HATE TO THINK WHAT YOU PUT IN YOUR TEA, MRS. MORROW

Elizabeth Morrow, poet, educator, and wife of Senator Dwight Morrow, invited the all-powerful banker J. P. Morgan to tea one day. Morgan possessed a huge, ugly nose that was almost as celebrated as his great wealth. Mrs. Morrow carefully coached her daughters not to comment on it, no matter how odd it might look to them. She was especially worried about what her daughter Anne might say. Anne, who later married Charles Lindbergh and became a best-selling writer, was known for speaking her mind. Anne couldn't take her eyes off Morgan's nose, but she and the other girls were quickly introduced to Morgan and ushered out of the room before they could do any damage. It was only then that Elizabeth Morrow relaxed her guard. "So, Mr. Morgan," she asked the esteemed guest, "will you have cream or lemon in your nose?"

RECYCLING

Although Arthur James, who taught classics at Eton for many years, could quote the great works of ancient Greece and Rome from memory, he was plagued by senior moments after his retirement. One day, when James was cycling home, he met a friend who noted that James had gotten a new bicycle. James looked down in confusion and realized that he must have taken the postmaster's bicycle by mistake. So he cycled to the post office, which was seven miles away, leaned the bicycle against the wall, went inside, apologized to the postmaster, went back outside, got back on the man's bicycle, and rode home.

OTHER THAN THAT,
I THINK I'M UP TO SPEED

When Prime Minister Benjamin Disraeli tried to visit his friend Lady Bradford, he was told by her servant that she had gone into town, as she usually did on Mondays. "I thought you would know that, sir," the servant said. "I did not," replied Disraeli, "nor did I know that it was Monday."

AT LEAST, I *THINK* HE'S DEAD

Senator Bob Dole's speech-making ability wasn't helped by his lapses of memory. He once sought to explain the difficulty faced by politicians intent on keeping their private lives private. "You read what Disraeli had to say," he declared, and then paused at some length. "I don't remember what he said. He said something." Another pause, then, "He's no longer with us."

YOU BETTER REMEMBER ME, YOU DIRTY RAT

When actor James Cagney saw a man across the street in New York, he said to his wife, "You see that fellow over there? He sat next to me in school. His name is Nathan Skidelsky." When his wife doubted his memory, Cagney went over to the man and—lo and behold—it *was* Nathan Skidelsky! However, for every prodigious feat of memory, there's a senior moment. In this case, it was Mr. Skidelsky who did not remember Cagney, one of the most famous actors in the world.

I WAS SO MUCH OLDER THEN, I'M EVEN OLDER THAN THAT NOW (FIRST VERSE)

Years after writing and recording the classic "Maggie Mae" in 1971, Rod Stewart revealed that the song had been inspired by his first true love—whose real name, alas, he could no longer remember.

OF COURSE, NO ONE'S
ACTUALLY GOING TO EAT IT

New York congressman Sol Bloom, an orthodox Jew, was running for reelection in 1924 when his friend New York senator Royal Copeland, a gentile, offered to help. At a big rally of Bloom's orthodox supporters, whose dietary laws prevent them from eating pork, Copeland was doing fine until he closed his speech by declaring, "And with your loyal support, I confidently predict that by this time tomorrow, your good friend and mine, Sol Bloom, will have brought home the bacon!"

IT'S A GOOD THING HE COULD
REMEMBER FLIGHT NUMBERS

In 1984 Dr. John Fellows bought a round-trip ticket from London to New York to pay a surprise visit to his daughter, who had just moved to the States. Unfortunately, the absentminded doctor could not remember his daughter's address upon landing. Nor her phone number. "I was tired," he explained later. And so he did what anyone suffering from an especially exhausting trip, coupled with an especially bad senior moment, would have done in the same situation: He caught the next plane home.

THAT IS TO SAY, YOUR *EX*–GOOD FRIEND ELLIOT MENDELSON

When the famously distracted Hungarian mathematician Paul Erdős met a colleague at a conference, Erdős asked the other man where he was from. "Vancouver," he replied. "Oh, then you must know my good friend Elliot Mendelson," Erdős remarked. His colleague gave him a funny look. "I *am* your good friend Elliot Mendelson!"

LOVELY THRONE, YOUR MAJESTY, BUT WHAT EXACTLY DOES THIS SWITCH DO?

When the Abyssinian emperor Menelek II decided to modernize his country in 1890, he personally ordered three electric chairs from New York, for truly modern executions. But it had slipped the emperor's mind that his country had no electricity. As a result, two of the chairs were quickly disposed of. The third, however, served nicely as the emperor's throne.

OH. THAT EXPLAINS WHY HE ASKED ME FOR A DOUBLE

In the 1920s movie star Douglas Fairbanks was driving back to his Beverly Hills estate when he passed a man with a familiar face and an aristocratic bearing who was walking down the road on a hot day. Fairbanks stopped to offer him a ride, which the surprised man accepted gratefully in an educated British accent. Unable to remember the man's name, but convinced he knew him from somewhere, Fairbanks invited

him inside his mansion
for a drink. During their
conversation, the visitor
seemed to know a lot of
Fairbanks's friends and was
even familiar with the mansion
itself, as if he had visited it often.
Fairbanks eventually managed to whisper
to his secretary, "Who is this Englishman?
I know he's Lord Somebody, but I can't
remember his name." "That," replied the
secretary, "is the English butler you fired
last month for getting drunk."

NEXT WEEK: FOOLPROOF TIPS
FOR REMEMBERING APPOINTMENTS

In 1984 the members of the Oxford
Library Club for Retired Professional
People and Others Interested were
especially looking forward to hearing a
guest speaker on the subject of "Old Age,
Absent-Mindedness, and Keeping Fit."
Unfortunately, the speaker forgot to turn up.

EXCEPT IN THE CASE OF PAINTINGS OF PROLETARIANS BEING CLUBBED BY THE RUNNING DOGS OF CAPITALISM

Mexican artist Diego Rivera was hired in 1933 to adorn Rockefeller Center's main lobby with a mural on the theme "Man at the Crossroads: Looking with Hope and High Vision to the Choosing of a New and Better Future." Rivera was one of the major figures in 20th-century art, but his hiring for this particular project in a bastion of American capitalism was the result of a costly senior moment on the part of Nelson Rockefeller, since Rivera was an internationally famous, outspoken communist. He put in scenes of the debauched rich in a nightclub, unemployed workers in a demonstration being clubbed by the police, and Lenin shaking hands with a Russian laborer and a black American worker. Rockefeller, who was in charge of interior decoration for the massive center, was mortified. Although Rivera agreed to change some controversial parts of the mural, he was adamant about not changing others. So Rockefeller ordered the immense, almost finished 63- by 17-foot fresco chipped off the wall. Years later, Rockefeller had another senior moment: "Art is probably one of the few areas left where there is complete freedom," he remarked.

AT LEAST I REMEMBERED THAT I FORGOT THEM

"Many years ago," Harpo Marx recalled late in life, "a very wise man named Bernard Baruch [the great financier and presidential adviser] took me aside and put his arm around my shoulder. 'Arthur, my boy,' he said, 'I'm going to give you three pieces of advice, three things you should always remember.' My heart jumped and I glowed with expectation. I was going to hear the magic passwords to a rich, full life from the master himself. 'Yes, sir?' I said. And he told me the three things. I regret that I've forgotten what they were."

A BRIDGE TOO FAR

In 1981 the Intermarine Company of Ameglia, Italy, landed an $8 million contract to build a minesweeper and three military launches for the Malaysian government. Only then did the people in charge of the project remember that the river connecting their shipyard to the sea was spanned by a very low bridge under which the ships would not be able to pass. The company offered to knock the bridge down and rebuild it after the ships were safely on their way, but the town refused, having grown more attached to the bridge than to the company.

AT LEAST HE DIDN'T DO THAT THING WHERE HE SHAKES THE WATER OFF

Philosopher Irwin Edman often used the pool of his friend and neighbor, publisher Robert Haas. One day, after finishing his laps, Edman wandered into Haas's living room and picked up a copy of *The History of the Peloponnesian War* by Thucydides. Forgetting that he was still in his wet bathing suit, the professor leafed through a few pages and then began to read. Later, after he'd left, Mrs. Haas arrived home. Furious, she called for the maid and pointed at the living room floor. "It's that dog again," she seethed. "No, Madame," the maid explained, "not the dog. It's the professor!"

WHEN I'M PRESIDENT, I SWEAR THIS SORT OF THING WON'T HAPPEN

Abraham Lincoln served as a captain during the Black Hawk War of 1832. One day he found himself leading a militia company across a field and toward a gate. The proper command for directing the troops through the gate escaped him completely. "This company is dismissed for two minutes," he finally shouted in desperation, "and will fall in again on the other side of the gate!"

. . . EXCEPT FOR FEBRUARY, WHICH HAS 37

Stolen license plates are often used to hide the identity of a car and, by extension, its driver. In Tennessee a drug dealer swiped a car with temporary cardboard plates, the kind used in some states until the metal ones arrive. But these particular cardboard plates had expired, as the date written on them clearly showed. So, using a pen, the dealer changed the plates' expiration date of 2-17-95 to one he thought was safely in the future: 2-37-95, obviously forgetting that months have 31 days, tops. Unfortunately, the cops who arrested him couldn't also charge him with aggravated senior moment.

WHERE THE TWO OF US WILL TALK ABOUT HOW CRAZY YOU ARE

Clergyman, writer, and famed wit Sydney Smith (1771–1845) described the English politician Lord Dudley Stuart as one of the most absentminded men he had ever met. "One day he met me in the street and invited me to meet myself: 'Dine with me today; dine with me, and I will get Sydney Smith to meet you.' I admitted the temptation he held out to me, but said I was engaged to meet him elsewhere."

HEY, IT'S HARD FOR A LINEMAN TO GET TO *ANY* END ZONE

In one of the greatest senior moments in sports history, Jim Marshall of the Minnesota Vikings snatched up a fumbled football in a game against the San Francisco 49ers on October 26, 1964, and started running the wrong way. That was bad enough, but on his 60-yard journey, Marshall didn't seem to grasp that his opponents showed no interest in stopping him. Worse, he ignored his own teammates, who raced after him shouting and motioning for him to turn around. When Marshall finally crossed his own team's goal line, scoring a safety—two points—for the other team, 49er Bruce Bosley hugged him.

FOR MY NEXT TRICK, I'LL BURY MYSELF IN THE WRONG GRAVE

The Irish writer Charles Maturin, famous for his horror stories, was also well known for his mental lapses. He was often seen wearing a boot on one foot and a shoe on the other, and sometimes turned up at parties one or two days late. He once sent a novel to his publishers in several packages, but neglected to include page numbers. It came as no surprise to his friends that his death in 1814 was hastened when he took the wrong medicine by mistake.

FLATTERY WILL GET YOU EVERYWHERE—OR AT LEAST OFF THE HOOK

When he was having a senior moment and couldn't place people, journalist Charles Michelson, FDR's speechwriter and the publicity director of the Democratic Party for 30 years, used this ploy to avoid offending them. When a person asked, "Do you remember me?" he would always answer, "Yes, and it turned out you were right, didn't it?"

NOT *ANOTHER* QUEEN!

In 1974, while taking a tour of Australia, which is part of the British Commonwealth, Prince Charles attended a service at a small parish church. After it was over, the cleric apologized for the small turnout: "Being a bank holiday weekend," he explained, "most of the parishioners are away." The prince was vexed. "Not another bank holiday!" he exclaimed, and then asked sarcastically what *this* one was in honor of. "Well," the rector replied, rather embarrassed, "over here we call it the queen's birthday."

THE VERY LONG GOOD-BYE

An absentminded young woman was about to take her leave of the essayist Agnes Repplier in the writer's Philadelphia apartment. At least it seemed that way to Repplier, who was sharper and wittier than most of her younger admirers when she died in 1950 in her nineties. Reluctant to leave, the visitor picked up her hat and scarf and then put them down again. She shifted her feet back and forth. She gazed around the room distractedly. Finally, she said, "There was something I meant to say, but I've forgotten what it was." "Perhaps, my dear," Repplier suggested helpfully, "it was good-bye."

AND IS COLONEL PANTS WELL?

Theodore Roosevelt prided himself on his memory for names and faces, although he was just as vulnerable to senior moments as anyone else. At a White House dinner one evening, he stood shaking hands with a long line of visitors.

When it was the turn of a man from New York who specialized in custom-made shirts, the haberdasher asked, "Do you remember me, Mr. President? I make your shirts." "Major Schurtz?" boomed Roosevelt, who had known the man for years. "Why, of course I remember, Major! And how are all the boys of the old regiment?"

THOSE WHO MISLAY THE PAST ARE DOOMED TO FORGET IT

Like many communities, Wilkinsburg, Pennsylvania, decided to prepare a time capsule for the people of the future. It was buried in 1962 and was supposed to be dug up 25 years later, during the town's centennial. But when 1987 rolled around, all the people involved in filling the capsule had died. Since they had also forgotten to write down its location, the ceremony to dig up the container had to be cancelled.

THE COLOR RED

In the film version of *The Color Purple*, the character played by Oprah Winfrey is knocked senseless with a pistol. As she lies on the ground, a puff of wind lifts her dress. The modest Ms. Winfrey, forgetting both that she was on camera and supposed to be unconscious, quickly pushes the dress down with her hand.

AND THE CHILDREN SHALL LEAD US

When the family of MIT mathematician Norbert Wiener moved from Cambridge, Massachusetts, to the nearby suburb of Newton, his wife knew the famously absentminded professor would never be able to find his way to the new place on his own. So she wrote down the Newton address on a piece of paper and gave it to him before he left that first morning. A few hours later, when an idea struck him, he found the piece of paper in his pocket and scribbled some notes on the back. After he looked the idea over, however, he decided it was worthless, and threw the paper away. With no note to remind him he had moved, he returned to his old house in Cambridge to be met by his daughter, waiting there for him. "Hi, Daddy," she said. "Mommy thought you would forget."

YOU CAN'T GO ON THE TRAIN AGAIN

Thomas Wolfe, author of the famous, posthumously published novel *You Can't Go Home Again,* was living in New York City in the early 1930s when he agreed to take a train to visit his editor, Maxwell Perkins, at Perkins's Connecticut home. As the train pulled out of Penn Station, Wolfe suddenly decided he'd rather stay in the city and write. Seized by a senior moment, he jumped off the train, sustaining injuries to both body and pride.

I'LL NEVER FORGET
WHAT'S-HER-NAME

When President Martin Van Buren wrote his autobiography in 1854, after he left office, he somehow forgot to mention his wife, the mother of his four sons, to whom he had been happily married for twelve years until her death in 1819.

STOP ME IF YOU'VE HEARD THE ONE
ABOUT ALL THE KING'S HORSES

Britain's Charles II, who reigned from 1660 to 1685, loved telling anecdotes about his past. His courtiers, who had heard the stories many times, found them so boring that they tried to escape if they could. The Earl of Rochester wondered how a man who could remember every last detail of a story couldn't recall that he had told it to the very same people the day before.

NO STARCH, AND MAKE SURE YOU TAKE EVERYTHING OUT OF THE POCKETS

Since the Cuban Missile Crisis in October of 1962, every U.S. president has been accompanied at all times by an armed military officer carrying an impenetrable titanium briefcase known as the "nuclear football." The briefcase contains the codes needed to launch a missile strike. The president also carries an "authenticator ID" that must be used in conjunction with the codes—unless, of course, he's forgotten where he put it. President Jimmy Carter did. He left it in the pocket of one of his suits, which was then sent to the dry cleaners.

TWO OUT OF THREE, MON AMI?

In 17th-century France, the Comte de Brancas was playing backgammon when he asked for a glass of wine. He proceeded to gulp down the dice and throw the wine on the board, soaking his opponent in the process.

TERRIBLY, TERRIBLY SORRY
ABOUT YOUR DEATH

Having attended the University of Edinburgh, Henry Erskine, Lord Advocate of Scotland in the late 18th century, would occasionally return to the university to visit his old friends. One day he met an especially absentminded, now elderly, tutor of whom he was very fond. He was taken aback when the man greeted him by saying, "I was very sorry, my dear boy, that you have had the fever in your family. Was it you or your brother who died of it?" Bemused, Erskine replied that it was he who had died. "Ah, dear me, I thought so," the tutor said sadly. "Very sorry for it," he kept muttering as he went on his way. "Very sorry for it."

NO HAIR
APPARENT

John Drew, a comic stage actor, once shaved off his mustache, dramatically changing his appearance. Soon after, he met Max Beerbohm, the English satirist, whom he failed to remember. Beerbohm, on the other hand, remembered the American. "Mr. Drew," he said, "I'm afraid you don't recognize me without your mustache."

OR MAYBE YOU SHOULD
GIVE POLITICS A TRY

In 1943 Warner Brothers released the musical comedy *This Is the Army,* written by Irving Berlin and costarring First Lieutenant Ronald Reagan. During the first week of shooting, Reagan was introduced to Berlin five different times, and Berlin said the same thing each time: "Young man, I just saw some of your work. You've got a few things to correct—for example, a huskiness of the voice—but you really should give this business some consideration when the war is over." Reagan had already been working in Hollywood for six years.

IT WAS, PERHAPS, THE BEST FAMILY I'VE EVER TASTED

Edward VII, Britain's king from 1901 to 1910, once tried to remember a visit he made to the home of Colonel James Biddle, during which he was served a dish of seasoned pork and cornmeal hardened into a loaf, then sliced and fried, known as scrapple. "In Philadelphia, when I was the Prince of Wales, I met a large and interesting family named Scrapple," he recalled hazily. "They served me a rather delicious native food, too—something, I believe, called Biddle."

I WAS SO MUCH OLDER THEN, I'M EVEN OLDER THAN THAT NOW (SECOND VERSE)

The rock and roll premature senility sweepstakes winner is . . . Mick Jagger! It was reported in 1968 that the Rolling Stones' lead singer, still only in his midtwenties, was forced to return a $5 million advance for his memoir because he couldn't remember enough about his own life.

WHEEEE!

In 1760 Belgian inventor Joseph Merlin attached steel wheels to his boots, thus creating the first pair of roller skates. To show off his new invention at a ball in London, he skated onto the dance floor while playing a violin. But he had forgotten to practice braking, and as a horrified observer recalled, Merlin "impelled himself against a mirror of more than five hundred pounds' value, dashed it to atoms, broke his instrument to pieces, and wounded himself most severely."

ON SECOND THOUGHT, I'LL SIT DOWN AND BE ASHAMED

On Disability Day in Texas, Gib Lewis, the Speaker of the State House of Representatives from 1983 to 1992, called out to a group of people in wheelchairs, "And now, will y'all stand and be recognized?"

DID I HAVE DESSERT?

Owner and publisher of the *New York Post* J. David Stern was walking down a Manhattan street in 1934 when he met a friend who suggested they have some lunch. Stern, who was pressed for time, reluctantly agreed, but only if they ate at a nearby restaurant. After they sat down and ordered, Stern wondered aloud why he wasn't hungry, at which point the waiter interjected, "I beg your pardon, sir, but you just finished lunch here five minutes ago."

WHILE WE'RE AT IT, LET'S CHANGE GRANTHAM TO . . . GRANTHAM!

In the late 1980s the town of Grantham, New Hampshire, sought to clear up the confusion that two streets with similar names, Stoney Brook Drive and Stoney Brook Lane, caused its residents. But the Grantham town council then forgot the point of renaming the streets in the first place, dubbing them Old Springs Drive and Old Springs Lane.

AH! THAT WOULD EXPLAIN THE STRANGE HAT I'M WEARING

Pope John XXIII, who was pontiff from 1958 until his death in 1963, once said that while he was falling asleep, important thoughts would drift through his mind and he would try to make a mental note: "I must speak to the pope about that." Then, he explained, "I would be wide awake and remember, 'I *am* the pope!'"

NOW, *THAT'S* ACTING

One day the famous British actor John Gielgud was dining in a restaurant with a well-known playwright when Gielgud spied someone he thought he recognized. "Did you see that man just coming in?" he asked his companion. "He's the biggest bore in London, second only to Edward Knoblock." It was precisely at that moment that he realized that the man sitting across from him was none other than Edward Knoblock. "Not you, of course," Gielgud quickly added. " I mean the *other* Edward Knoblock."

AND THAT'S SPELLED L-A-M-P-E

After German philosopher Immanuel Kant fired his long-time servant, Lampe, he feared that the man would remain in his memory forever. A little guilt, perhaps? So Kant wrote in his journal, "Remember in the future the name of Lampe must be completely forgotten."

NO DOMESTIC PAWN

In 1937 chess master George Koltanowski simultaneously defeated 34 players while blindfolded, a world record. But when he died, his wife Leah said that Koltanowski had never once remembered to bring home bread from the grocery.

HOW CAN I BE SURE?

Jesse Lasky, whose career as a Hollywood producer and studio executive stretched from 1913 to 1951, was making a speech

welcoming Maurice Chevalier at a dinner in
New York when he kept losing his place.
Each time he looked up in confusion and
said, "Now where was I?" He did this so
many times that comedian George Jessel
finally called out, "You're at the Hotel
Astor and your name is Jesse Lasky."

MENTAL ERROR ON THE PITCHER

When Atlanta Braves pitcher Charlie
Liebrandt struck out his thousandth
batter in a game against the Philadelphia
Phillies, he wanted to keep the ball as a
souvenir. When the catcher threw it back
to him, Liebrandt tossed the ball into the
dugout, expecting to get it later. One thing,
however, had slipped his mind: He hadn't
asked the umpire to call a time-out.
Watching as the ball rolled into the dugout,
the Phillie on first ran safely to second
base, and Liebrandt was charged with
an error.

TO SAY NOTHING OF THE FACT THAT EVERYONE WAS WEARING A DARK SUIT

The two men who set out to rob the AmeriSuites Hotel in Little Rock, Arkansas, forgot to do their homework. When they tried to stick up the night clerk, they discovered that the hotel was the temporary home of a large contingent of Secret Service agents who were protecting President-Elect Bill Clinton and Vice President–Elect Al Gore after the 1992 election. The robbers also forgot to take a close look at the parking lot, which alone should have been a dead giveaway. It was full of government vehicles with emergency lights and District of Columbia plates.

THE WORD IS "CONFUSED"

Allen Ludden, the host of the TV word-association game show *Password*, had a senior moment on the air that must have confused even the most adept puzzle solver: "Just remember, folks," he announced, "next Monday night's *Password* will be seen on Thursday evening."

I'D LIKE TO MEET THAT MAN SOME DAY

Franz Schubert's friends were amazed that he often seemed to be in a trance when he wrote and afterward did not remember what he had done. One day the tenor Vogel sang one of Schubert's songs, and when he was finished, Schubert exclaimed, "That's not bad! Who wrote it?"

AND WHENEVER I SAY ST. PAUL, I'LL MEAN MINNEAPOLIS

Dr. William Archibald Spooner, the absentminded Anglican priest and Oxford University administrator who gave his name to the linguistic lapses called "spoonerisms," once concluded a sermon by stating, "In the sermon I have just preached, whenever I said Aristotle, I meant St. Paul."

THOSE WHO FORGET HISTORY
ARE CONDEMNED TO CONDEMN
PERFECTLY NICE BUILDINGS

The Lower East Side Tenement Museum, on Orchard Street in Manhattan, was created in 1988 to honor the lives of millions of immigrants who lived in the city's overcrowded tenements. These dark, narrow buildings were decried by reformers as early as 1843 for being defective in size, arrangement, warmth, ventilation, and sanitation. If tenants complained, they were immediately evicted. Flash forward to 2002, when the Tenement Museum's board members were suffering a curious memory lapse, forgetting the very history they wanted visitors to remember. In order to expand, they struck an agreement with the state to have the building next door condemned—even though it had recently been renovated. The plan was to evict the tenants, just as in the bad old days, and then spend more than $2 million to expand the museum by re-creating a slum out of the modernized building. As Ruth J. Abram, the museum's president, admitted, "It does seem ironic." Deepening the irony, the ancestors of the building's owner, Lou Holzman, had been immigrants themselves and began living in the building in 1910. After a storm of bad publicity, the state tabled the idea.

AND THEN I PUT MY HEAD THROUGH THE WINDSHIELD, JUST FOR THE HELL OF IT

The year 1977 was a big one for senior moments involving Canadian drivers. According to the *Toronto Sun,* one driver, filling out an insurance claim form, explained his mishap this way: "Coming home I drove into the wrong house and collided with a tree I don't have." Another unfortunate driver wrote on his claim form, "I thought my window was down but I found out that it was up when I put my head through it."

LOOK, HONEY, THE DRESSER
I BOUGHT COMES WITH A BRAIN!

After the death of the beloved 18th-century French author and philosopher Voltaire, his heart and brain were removed and preserved as national treasures. His heirs and the government fought for years over the body parts' ultimate disposition; in the meantime the brain, it's believed, was accidentally placed in a chest of drawers. Later no one could remember which chest it was, only that it had been among a number of other pieces of furniture that were sold to unknown bidders at auction. Strangely, the "lucky" bidder never reported the brain he found in one of the drawers. (Voltaire's heart, however, lies safely in the Bibliothèque Nationale in Paris.)

ON THE WHOLE,
I'D RATHER BE IN THE BLACK

Terrified of finding himself in a strange city without money, W. C. Fields opened a bank account in every town he visited. Moreover, he used a different name for each account because he was fearful of being robbed. Unfortunately, because he never bothered to write down the aliases, he eventually forgot all but 23 of them—out of an estimated 700.

GENERAL MEMORY LOSS

Sir William Erskine was a senior commander under the Duke of Wellington. During one of Erskine's more appalling senior moments, he was found eating dinner instead of defending a strategic bridge. He later had second thoughts about neglecting the bridge, but dispatched only five men. When another officer expressed his concern, Erskine changed his mind again and decided he would send an entire regiment. He wrote a note to himself as a reminder, put it in his pocket, and then forgot all about it.

IT COULD HAVE BEEN WORSE—
HE COULD HAVE LEFT OUT
THE SECOND "H"

In 1995 Dan O'Connor, a rabid Notre Dame football fan, decided to have the team's slogan, "Fighting Irish," tattooed on his arm. But the tattoo artist, who was paid $125, picked the wrong time to have a senior spelling moment. Even with the design right in front of him, he inscribed the words, "Fighing Irish." O'Connor, who filed a suit for damages, reportedly said, "You're not talking about a dented car where you can get another one. You're talking about flesh."

THE THIRD ANNUAL
G. K. CHESTERTON AWARD
FOR ABSENTMINDEDNESS
GOES TO . . . G. K. CHESTERTON!

English writer G. K. Chesterton was especially baffled by trains. He once went up to a ticket window at a railroad station and asked the mystified agent for a cup of coffee, then retired to the station restaurant to wait for his train and tried to buy a ticket from the waiter.

AND WE WERE SO DESPERATE, WE DIDN'T EVEN BOTHER TO READ THEM FIRST

Entrepreneur Richard Branson, the founder of Virgin Records, Virgin Atlantic Airways, Virgin Express, and Virgin Mobile, is famous for his love of adventure. Having forgotten to take one essential item on an around-the-world balloon expedition, he offered this advice to fellow thrill-seekers: "If you're embarking around the world in a hot-air balloon, don't forget the toilet paper. Once, we had to wait for incoming faxes."

I THINK I SHALL NEVER SEE /
A POEM AS LOVELY AS A SOCK

Reverend William Lisle Bowles, a friend of the Lake Poets, the group that included Coleridge and Wordsworth, was a minor poet himself, but, according to his peers, his most distinguishing characteristic was his forgetfulness. One evening he gave a dinner party for friends, only to keep them waiting downstairs. When his wife went up to fetch him, she found him searching everywhere for a sock to put on his bare foot. After joining the search, she discovered that he had put two socks on the other foot while thinking about a new poem.

DO NOT TAKE YOUR EYES
OFF MY PLUME, SOLDIER,
AND THAT'S AN ORDER

Alexander Borodin was a general in the Russian Army, as well as being a famous composer, chemist, and doctor. He once walked out of his home in full military dress. His jacket was adorned with medals and he wore a plumed helmet and everything else necessary for a full dress parade—except, that is, his pants.

AND THAT'S WHEN I FIGURED OUT THAT WRITING THE WORDS WAS GOING TO BE EASIER THAN REMEMBERING THEM

The English novelist Paul Baily was once an actor, playing in *Richard III* at Stratford-upon-Avon, with Christopher Plummer in the leading role. In Act III, Scene V, Baily, playing the role of Lovell, was supposed to say, "Here is the head of that ignoble traitor, the dangerous and unsuspected Hastings." One night he couldn't remember the line at all. Plummer stared at him "for what seemed like ten minutes," Baily said in 1996, and then declared, "Is that the head of that ignoble traitor, the dangerous and unsuspected Hastings?" To which the grateful Baily replied, to everyone's relief, "Yes."

GIVE OR TAKE A FEW ZEROS

Something must have slipped the collective mind of New York investment firm Bear Stearns when in 2002 it ordered the sale of $4 billion worth of stock instead of the correct amount, $4 million, a 1,000-fold mistake. After its hideously expensive senior moment, the company was able to recover only about 85% of the mistakenly sold stock. And to think that a Bear Stearns advertisement had just boasted of the firm's ability to "execute complex transactions flawlessly."

NICE TRY

Confederate Colonel Robert Martin had a unique plan to conquer the Union during the Civil War. With the help of eight secret agents, he would burn New York City to the ground on the cold night of November 25, 1864. The men checked into various hotels, quickly lit small fires, assuming they would spread, and then fled.

But they had forgotten one critical fact: Fires need oxygen. The agents had neglected to open the windows and doors. Starved of oxygen, the fires eventually petered out without spreading, and New York and the Union were left standing.

WHAT ARE YOU SAYING— THAT NEWSPAPERS DON'T DELIVER THEMSELVES?

In 1965 publisher Lionel Burleigh launched the *Commonwealth Sentinel,* which, he claimed, would be "Britain's most fearless newspaper." Burleigh was staying at London's Brown Hotel, frantically preparing for the paper's debut, when he received a call from the police: "Do you have anything to do with the *Commonwealth Sentinel*? Because there are 50,000 [copies] outside the hotel entrance and they're blocking the street." It seems that Burleigh had completely forgotten to arrange for the paper's distribution. As a result, the *Sentinel,* which was born on February 6, 1965, died on February 7.

OUR ACCOUNTANTS
ADVISED US NOT TO

Companies in Washington, D.C., mailed, as usual, their quarterly tax payments that were due on September 30, 1994, to a special post office box, only to have their envelopes returned, stamped "Box Closed for Nonpayment of Rent." It seems that government officials had forgotten to pay the $405 annual fee needed to keep the boxes open.

YEAH, BUT SEE HOW NICELY
THE GLOVE COMPARTMENT
OPENS AND CLOSES

Former General Motors executive and automotive engineer John DeLorean's senior moment was one of the most expensive in history. Determined to strike out on his own, in 1981 he brought to life the DeLorean, a sports car modestly named after himself. Alas, this brilliant man suffered a series of senior moments about, among other things, the importance of well-designed parts, lightweight materials, and low-cost manufacturing. His car featured gull-wing doors that were hard to open and close, the body was too heavy, the engine wasn't powerful enough, and visibility was poor. Only about 9,000 cars were made, and the company's investors lost millions.

I KNEW THERE WAS SOMETHING VAGUELY FAMILIAR ABOUT ALL THAT BRILLIANT PROSE

When the absentminded Scottish writer John Campbell (1708–1775) was in a bookstore one day, he became so engrossed in a book that it wasn't until he bought it, took it home, and read it halfway through that he realized he himself had written it.

AND NOW I WILL FREE
ALL CONVICTED MURDERERS
ON THE GROUNDS THAT THEY MERELY
FAILED TO COMPLY WITH THE LAWS
PROHIBITING THE KILLING OF OTHERS

When former New York mayor David Dinkins was accused of failing to pay his taxes, he blamed his poor memory. He had merely forgotten to do it, he explained, which made his sin one of omission, not commission—and thus not worth bothering about. "I haven't committed a crime," he stated forcefully. "What I did was fail to comply with the law."

JUST DON'T LET HIM
TOUCH THE GROUND

For a 1994 meeting the members of the Republican caucus of Grand Rapids, Michigan, forgot to bring the American flag for the obligatory Pledge of Allegiance. The members were stymied until party member Jack Pettit, who happened to be wearing a Stars-and-Stripes necktie, climbed onto a chair and remained motionless while everyone recited the words.

THANKS, BUT I ALREADY HAVE A BOOKMARK JUST LIKE IT

When Albert Einstein received a $1,500 check from the Rockefeller Foundation as an honorarium, he used it as a bookmark for months, then lost the book. Trying to keep its records in order, the Foundation sent a duplicate check, and Einstein, having forgotten the first one, wrote back, "What's this for?"

NEXT STOP: AMNESIAVILLE

Traveling by train to attend a ceremony, the bishop of Exeter, William Cecil, couldn't find his ticket. "It's all right, my Lord," said the sympathetic collector. "We know who you are." "That's all very well," replied the bishop, "but without my ticket, how am I to know where I'm going?"

ANOTHER ROUND OF GROG, MATEY, AND WE MIGHT GET A STANDING O.

Actor Alan Devlin was known for his habit of leaving the stage in a fit of pique in midperformance. Once, while appearing in *H.M.S. Pinafore* at the Dublin Gaiety Theatre in 1987, he looked out at the audience and shouted, "I'm going home! Finish it yourself!" But first he took a detour. He went to Neary's bar in his admiral's costume and ordered a round of drinks. But Devlin had forgotten to take off his radio mike, which was still turned on, so the sounds of alcohol-fueled conversation and clinking glasses filled the theater as the dumbfounded cast and audience listened in.

THANK GOD WE FOUND A GAS STATION THAT WAS OPEN

When two robbers knocked off a gas station in Vancouver, Canada, in 1981, they locked the attendant in the bathroom and drove off with $100. After

driving around for a while, they realized
they were lost and pulled back into the
same station to ask for directions, failing
to recognize either it or the attendant,
who had just escaped from the bathroom.
As they left the station for the second time,
the attendant called the police. Amazingly,
the memory-impaired thieves then returned
for a *third time*—now on foot. Their car
had broken down a short distance away,
they said, and they needed a tow.

USUALLY I HANG AROUND PURGATORY. YOU?

Patrick John Ryan, the archbishop of
Philadelphia, was once accosted on
the street by a man in the devilish grip of a
senior moment. The stranger was absolutely
certain he had seen the archbishop's face
before but couldn't remember who he was.
"Now where in hell have I seen you?"
the man asked, growing more and more
frustrated. The archbishop replied,
"From where in hell do you come?"

IF YOU HUM A FEW BARS, MAYBE I'LL REMEMBER WHERE I PUT IT

A lexander Borodin's most famous musical work was the opera *Prince Igor,* but soon after he began it, his mind wandered, and he used the music for a symphony instead. From time to time over the years, he would write an aria for *Prince Igor,* but he invariably forgot to put it into the opera and moved on to something else. Finally fellow Russian composer Rimsky-Korsakov finished *Prince Igor* for him—three years after Borodin's death.

NAME ANOTHER PARTY

B efore winning a senate seat in North Carolina in 1998, future vice presidential candidate John Edwards showed little interest in politics and often forgot to vote. He was once asked whether he had started his political life by registering as a Democrat or Republican. He couldn't remember.

I'VE JUST HAD THE MOST WONDERFUL CONVERSATION WITH 894-606-5789

The brilliant Hungarian mathematician Paul Erdős had the habit of phoning colleagues around the world at all times of the day. Although he could remember the phone number of every mathematician he knew, he frequently couldn't recall their first names, so he didn't use them in conversation—except for that of one colleague, Tom Trotter, whom he called Bill.

ON THE OTHER HAND, I CAN HEAR A GUN COCKING 26 MILES AWAY

President Ulysses S. Grant had no ear for music, and no memory for it, either. When he was asked one evening if he had enjoyed a concert, he replied, "How could I? I know only two tunes. One of them is 'Yankee Doodle' and the other one isn't."

THOU SHALT REMEMBER!

Bill Harbach, one of the first executive
producers of *The Tonight Show*, once
attempted to ask his secretary to telephone
future guest Charlton Heston to arrange a
rehearsal. "Get me . . . uh . . . Charleston
Huston!" Harbach barked. "Wait—I, uh,
mean Charlton Hudson!" Suddenly recalling
that the actor had starred as Moses in
the movie *The Ten Commandments*, he
corrected himself. "You know who I mean!"
he told his secretary. "Chester Moses."

YOU THINK THIS IS BAD?
YOU SHOULD SEE WHAT I'M LIKE
WITH PARISHIONERS!

In the 18th century English vicar George
Harvest was frequently forced to borrow
a horse when he traveled, because he had
forgotten where he left his own. Eventually,
people stopped lending him theirs because
he mislaid those, too. When he did have his
animal with him, he would dismount when
he arrived at his destination and lead it

away. But if the horse shook off the bridle or a stable boy removed it, the oblivious parson would continue to walk, holding the reins as if the horse were still attached.

WHAT ABOUT THE PAINTING OF THAT WOMAN WITH THE ENIGMATIC SMILE? DON'T TELL ME I OWN THAT ONE, TOO!

Eccentric publishing magnate William Randolph Hearst (1863 1951) was famous for his fanatical pursuit of art, which Orson Welles satirized in his film *Citizen Kane.* Once, Hearst sent an assistant to scour Europe for a masterpiece he was determined to add to his collection. Several months later, after he had looked everywhere, the man reported back that he'd finally located the item, and it would cost Hearst nothing! Why? Because the publisher had already bought it years before, stored it in a warehouse overseas, and then, as he had done with so many other things, forgotten all about it.

AND, INCIDENTALLY, YOU WOULDN'T HAVE ANY IDEA WHAT PART I'M PLAYING, WOULD YOU?

Actor Junius Booth, the father of Lincoln assassin John Wilkes Booth and actor Edwin Booth, was famous for his senior moments. One time he was backstage when he ran into the theater manager, who was anxiously looking for him just before the curtain was supposed to go up. "Where's the stage?" Booth asked, then added, "And what's the play?"

NOW WHAT KIND OF LOWLIFE WOULD ROB SOMEONE'S CAR?

In 1997 Paco Bocconini snatched the equivalent of $4,500 from a post office in Cariato, Italy. But when he raced outside to jump into his getaway car, the car was nowhere to be found. It seems he had forgotten to turn off the engine and the car had been stolen. He was still standing in front of the post office when the police arrived.

AH, AND THAT WOULD EXPLAIN WHY YOU'RE WEARING THE MORE EXPENSIVE SUIT

Maxwell Perkins (1884–1947), the influential editor of F. Scott Fitzgerald, Ernest Hemingway, and Thomas Wolfe, was talking to a young writer one day when a distinguished-looking man entered Perkins's office at Charles Scribner's Sons, the New York publishing house. Perkins looked up at the man with no sign of recognition. Finally, the visitor could stand it no longer. "I'm Charles Scribner," Perkins's employer snapped.

NOW, DON'T YOU FEEL BETTER?

Tatiana Cooley, the winner of several national memory contests, can remember a list of 3,125 words, 100 names and faces, 1,000 numbers, a 54-line poem, and the precise order of a shuffled deck of cards. But when it comes to everyday life, she's notoriously absentminded and is a chronic user of Post-it notes and shopping lists.

AND MY NAME IS . . .
SEÑOR MOMENTO!

For a performance of Puccini's opera *Turandot,* the Rome Opera designed a set with a little stream and a small Chinese bridge that crossed over it. On one side of the stream was Carlos Gasparini, the tenor playing Prince Calaf, and on the other side, the soprano who played Princess Turandot. When she cried *"Mio nome è Amore!"* ("My name is love!"), he was supposed to run across the bridge and embrace her, but he forgot and tried to leap across the stream instead, tripped, and fell in.

YOU REALLY GOT ME SO I DON'T
KNOW WHAT I'M DOING

When rock star Ray Davies of the Kinks took his driving test in the 1960s, he forgot to look where he was going and knocked down a woman carrying groceries. He jumped out of the car to help her, but forgot to put on the

parking brake, forcing the driving instructor
to stop the moving car before it could do any
more damage. "I was only learning to drive
because I thought I should be a regular
person," Davies said. "But that was stupid."

AND WHERE ARE CO-CHAIRMEN
LARRY AND SHEMP?

President Ronald Reagan's senior
moments were legendary. He often
forgot what foreign country
he was in or the name of the
dignitary he was meeting.
When he visited Brazil, he
referred to it as Bolivia. He
greeted Princess Diana as
"Princess David"; at a conference of
mayors once introduced himself to Samuel
Pierce, the only African-American member
of his cabinet, who he thought was the mayor
of some American city; and called President
Samuel Doe of Liberia "Chairman Moe."

TOTALLY WINGING IT

The Irish-born American stage actress Ada Rehan (1857–1916) once played a heroine in a romantic comedy opposite a nervous young actor. During one scene she asked him a question that was crucial to the plot and then paused to wait for his answer. But the actor had forgotten his line, which was, literally, "You don't reply." Someone in the wings frantically prompted him: "You don't reply. . . . You don't reply." The young man, who was at his wit's end, thought it was a stage direction. He exclaimed with great irritation, "Well, how the hell can I reply, when I don't know what to say?"

AND HE'S BEEN DEAD FOR CENTURIES

After Daniel Webster's death, Congressman Jerry Simpson of Kansas eulogized the great Massachusetts senator, orator, and lawyer. However,

at one point he confused Daniel with Noah
Webster (no relation) and praised the
latter's dictionary, the first one written and
published by an American. A congressman
next to him whispered, "*Noah* made the
dictionary," to which Simpson, his mind
plunging deeper into his senior moment,
whispered back, "Noah built the *Ark!*"

HIGH-HEELED-SHOE-IN-MOUTH DISEASE

New York congressman Clarence E.
Hancock was one of several speakers
at a meeting of a women's club in his
district. Hancock, who served in the
House for 20 years, was introduced by
the club's chairwoman: "Members, this is
our last meeting of the year," she began,
"and we have enjoyed a splendid program.
Our speakers have been both entertaining
and instructive. But today we have
something quite different. I present
Congressman Hancock."

THE FIRST VIRTUE IS NOT BEING ABLE TO REMEMBER VIRTUES

On his eightieth birthday, writer Somerset Maugham spoke at a dinner held in his honor in London. "There are many virtues in growing old," he began, but then stopped and stared down at the table. The pause grew into a long, awkward silence. Maugham looked absently around the room, shifting from foot to foot, glancing helplessly at his notes. Finally, he cleared his throat and explained, "I'm just trying to think what they are."

16. LEAVE LIST IN CAR SO POLICE CAN CATCH US

In 1996 two escaped prisoners from Marble Valley, Vermont, were forced to abandon a stolen car when a police officer approached them. Inside was a very helpful list the forgetful fugitives wrote to help them remember what to do: "Drive to Maine, get safer place to stay, buy guns, get Marie, get car—Dartmouth, do robbery, go to New York." The prisoners were later picked up in Manhattan getting off a Maine-to-New-York bus.

WHAT A COINCIDENCE! IT HAS THE SAME NAME AS I DO!

While working with certain equations, the great mathematician David Hilbert suggested a revolutionary idea that led to the development of a new kind of geometry. It involved multidimensional spaces that came to be known as "Hilbert spaces." Some time later, Hilbert attended a conference with fellow mathematician Richard Courant. Several papers presented there referred to this or that Hilbert space. After one such presentation, a genuinely puzzled Hilbert turned to his colleague and asked, "Richard, exactly what is a Hilbert space?"

CUSTOMERS REALLY CLEANED UP

In 1992, as a promotional gimmick, the British division of the Hoover vacuum cleaner company offered two free, round-trip airline tickets from London to other European cities. All you had to do in order to qualify was buy $150 worth of Hoover products. If you bought $375 worth, you got two free round-trip tickets to New York or Orlando. Apparently people at the company had forgotten to do the math. More than 20,000 customers got free tickets before Hoover ended the promotional campaign, having lost $50 million.

YOU KNOW, IT'S THAT AMERICAN PHILOSOPHICAL MOVEMENT CONCERNED WITH SPIRITUALITY . . .

Essayist, poet, and philosopher Ralph Waldo Emerson attended the funeral of his good friend Henry Wadsworth Longfellow in 1882, but the absentminded Emerson couldn't recall Longfellow's name. When he turned to a fellow mourner, he referred to his friend as "That gentleman," and then added, "had a sweet, beautiful soul." Emerson often forgot the names of inanimate objects, as well, and had to refer to them in a roundabout way. "The implement that cultivates the soil" was a plow and "the thing that strangers take away" was an umbrella.

NOBODY'S PERFECT

On July 28, 1962, the *Mariner 1* space probe was launched from Cape Canaveral. Its scientific mission: to reach Venus after 100 days in space, go into orbit, and then send back valuable data. But four minutes after the launch, the $18 million rocket veered dangerously off course and had to be destroyed by remote control. The cause? Someone had forgotten to put one symbol into the computer's program.

BUT WE'RE PRETTY SURE IT ISN'T FLAT

The original 1970s proposal for the multibillion-dollar "Star Wars" satellite and nuclear missile shield had to be revised when the scientists working on the project suffered an extraordinary memory lapse. Incredibly elaborate calculations were needed for a network of satellites to have any chance of detecting enemy missiles in midflight so they could be destroyed by our antimissile missiles before reaching the U.S. Unfortunately, the scientists forgot to take into consideration the precise dimensions of Earth, making it impossible to gauge the likely path and position of any of the warheads.

SAY YOU'LL CALL BACK—WE'RE IN THE MIDDLE OF A PLAY

Actor A. E. Mathews's memory deserted him at the most inopportune times. Matthews (1869–1960) once appeared in a play involving a telephone call that was critical to the plot. It was a call that

Mathews was supposed to answer, but when the phone rang on cue and Mathews picked up the receiver, his mind went blank. Desperate, he turned to the other actor on stage and said, "It's for you."

UNTIL TOTAL AMNESIA DO US PART

In 1920 Albert Muldoon agreed to be the best man for his friend Christopher at a marriage ceremony in Kileter, a village in Northern Ireland. But having forgotten where to stand during the ceremony, he wound up on the wrong side of the groom. The priest, never having laid eyes on the happy couple, addressed Muldoon during the service instead of Christopher. Muldoon, by now thoroughly muddled, dutifully answered the priest's questions while Christopher suffered his own senior moment, having forgotten how the ceremony was supposed to go. It was only when Muldoon was poised to sign his name in the registry under the heading of "Groom" that the bride realized she was about to marry the wrong man.

AND TO THINK I'M *STILL* GOING TO THE HALL OF FAME

In the first decade of the last century, pitcher Rube Waddell of the Philadelphia Athletics, perhaps the most eccentric baseball player in history, often wandered off between innings when he was supposed to be in the dugout. Once, after a frantic search, teammates found him shooting marbles with some local kids behind the ballpark; another time, he left to chase a fire truck. He sometimes arrived just a few minutes before game time, made his way through the stands, and jumped onto the field, tearing off his clothes as he approached the clubhouse to change into his uniform.

GET SHAKESPEARE— WE NEED A REWRITE!

For a Columbia Pictures film about big business, a screenwriter needed an important speech for the CEO to deliver to his board of directors. So he picked one that Spartacus, the Roman slave turned rebel leader, had made to his followers. "What the hell is this?" Columbia head Harry Cohen exploded when he read the script. The screenwriter explained where the speech came from, but Cohen wasn't buying it. "I don't want any of that crap," he said impatiently. "I want a speech that everyone in the audience will recognize immediately." "You mean like Hamlet's soliloquy?" asked the screenwriter. "No! No!" yelled Cohen, who was known for his terrible temper and his equally bad memory. "I mean something like 'To be or not to be!'"

I THINK I SAW
MARIEL HEMINGWAY WITH IT

They call it the greatest honor an actor can receive, but even an Oscar cannot withstand the power of a senior moment. During the 1979 Academy Awards ceremony, Meryl Streep left her statue for Best Supporting Actress on the back of a toilet in the ladies' room. (Fortunately, it was recovered later.)

INDELIBLY YOURS

James J. Sylvester, a professor at Johns Hopkins University in the 19th century, was notoriously absentminded. One afternoon, just as one of his students was going out for a walk, Sylvester handed him an ink bottle and asked him to drop it in the letterbox, since he was very anxious to have an immediate reply.

AND, FURTHERMORE, ONCE YOU TELL ME, I'LL DISAGREE WITH YOU EVEN MORE!

The 19th-century English novelist Anthony Trollope worked for the post office most of life. It was his habit of waking very early and writing at great speed before leaving for the office that likely brought on this senior moment: At a staff meeting one day, Trollope snapped at a colleague who had spoken before him, "I disagree with you entirely! What was it you said?"

EXCEPT FOR THAT, I THINK
WE'RE IN PRETTY GOOD SHAPE

In Cuba in 1898 during the Spanish-American War, U.S. soldiers charging up San Juan Hill were quickly confronted with barbed wire, a typical first line of defense. But no one had remembered to bring wire cutters. Artillery support, which is also a given in an infantry assault, had been forgotten as well.

WHOSE SIDE ARE YOU ON?

In 2002 officials of Teamsters Local 988 of Houston, Texas, must have forgotten they were running a union. They built a new meeting hall using nonunion labor. They then compounded their memory lapse by responding to a reporter's request for an on-the-record explanation with the statement, "Union workers cost too much."

I'M AFRAID IT WILL JUST BE YOU
TONIGHT, MONSIEUR BONAPARTE

André-Marie Ampère, the great French physicist, was invited to dine with the most powerful man in the world, Emperor Napoleon. He forgot all about it and never showed up.

PLEASE HAVE THAT MAN
REMOVED AT ONCE

The great conductor Arturo Toscanini (1867–1957) would often sing along with the orchestra during rehearsals. But sometimes he would forget what he was doing. Once, during a dress rehearsal, his voice was so loud that it could be heard above the instruments. Suddenly he stopped the orchestra. "For the love of God," he snapped, "who's singing here?"

ON THE OTHER HAND,
I'LL BE BORED OUT OF MY MIND

One Sunday George Salmon, a 19th-century Regius professor of divinity at Trinity College, Dublin, absentmindedly brought to church the same sermon he had preached the year before. Unable to think of anything else to do, he pressed on, reading from the text. He later explained his reasoning this way: that half the congregation had surely not been in church back then, so it was new to them; that one quarter *had* heard the sermon, but was just as absentminded as he was, and no doubt had forgotten it altogether; and that the final quarter of the congregation would be happy to hear it again regardless.

DAMN! I *KNEW* I SHOULDN'T HAVE MISSED THE LAST SIX REHEARSALS

A t an American performance of Verdi's opera *Ernani* in 1847, the tenor, playing a bandit of noble descent, made a grand entrance from stage left only to find that the rest of the cast was facing stage right, waiting for him to appear. Then he tried to pull out his sword for his big aria, only to have it get stuck in the scabbard. When he finally got it out, he couldn't get it back in. By now completely desperate, he raced for the stage exit, only to discover that he had picked the wrong one. It was nailed shut.

BUT AT LEAST WE WERE ABLE TO PLAY BACKGAMMON WHILE WE EXPIRED

N ineteenth-century English explorer John Franklin trudged through the frozen wastes of the Arctic accompanied by 129 men, who carried, among other things, a backgammon game, books, and polish for brass buttons. On the other hand, they

forgot to bring rifles. Unable to shoot any game for food, they all starved to death.

AND A TRIUMPH OF FORGETFULNESS!

Actor Paul Greenwood made senior-moment history in July 1984, when he performed on the London stage in the play *The Happiest Days of Your Life* on opening night. At the very beginning of the first scene, he was supposed to write down a note, but he couldn't find a pencil or pen in his pocket. There was dead silence in the theater as the audience waited for something to happen. When Greenwood finally recovered his power of speech, it was clear that he had completely forgotten his lines. He proceeded to make them up, although he did try to follow the general thrust of the play. In the third act, he asked the audience, "Shall I start again?" Amazed by the entire evening, they shouted back "Yes!" In its review, *The Times* of London called it "memory loss on a grand scale."

ALSO, I'D FILM MYSELF
ONLY IN CLOSE-UP

One day movie mogul Cecil B. DeMille found himself directing a scene in which a cowboy was supposed to fall off his horse after a rifle shot. "No matter what happens," DeMille told the cameraman, "I want you to keep filming. Don't stop for anything." The scene began perfectly, but it was so realistic that a studio doctor, new to the ways of Hollywood, thought that the cowboy had actually been injured. He raced onto the set to give him first aid, ruining the rest of the shot. An enraged DeMille jumped up and ran after him, shaking his fist and cursing so vociferously that the doctor fled. When DeMille watched the rushes later, he was surprised to see the doctor dash into the scene pursued by a bald man shaking his fists and cursing. "Who in the world is that?" DeMille asked, genuinely puzzled. "That's the studio doctor," an assistant replied. "No,"

DeMille said. "I meant the other man who was using such foul language." "That, sir, is you," the assistant explained. "Young man," DeMille declared, "that may appear to be me, but I assure you it is not. I never use language like that."

GENIUS GETS GIRL, GENIUS LOSES GIRL, GENIUS FINDS GIRL, GENIUS LOSES TICKET

In late 1930 Albert Einstein left Berlin to visit the United States. The Einstein Archive contains the following summation of a page reproduced from his travel diary: "The page depicted here describes the hectic departure of Einstein and his wife Elsa from the railway station in Berlin, 30 November 1930. First he loses his wife, finds her again, and then he loses the tickets and finds them as well. Thus began Einstein's second trip to the U.S."

THE FOURTH ANNUAL
G. K. CHESTERTON AWARD
FOR ABSENTMINDEDNESS
GOES TO . . . G. K. CHESTERTON!

The wife of writer G. K. Chesterton grew accustomed to the breathtaking variety of her husband's senior moments. Once, when he was taking a bath, she heard him get out of the tub. After a long pause, there was a loud splash. It turned out that Chesterton had forgotten what he was doing and climbed back into the tub. When he realized his mistake, he cried out, "Damn, I've been here before!"

STAMP OUT
GEOGRAPHICAL ILLITERACY

In 1999 the U.S. Postal Service printed a set of 60-cent stamps with a picture of the Grand Canyon. The stamps read "Grand Canyon, Colorado." The Grand Canyon is in Arizona.

THIS SHOULD DO THE TRICK

In 1989 Barry Buchstaber was standing beside a car that had two broken windows when a San Mateo County, California, deputy sheriff asked him for identification. Buchstaber absentmindedly handed him the one official-looking document he had: a copy of an arrest warrant sworn out against him for driving with a suspended license.

I FORGET WHAT THEY CALL IT WHEN YOUR SENIOR MOMENT LASTS A DECADE

David Bowie once said that he could no longer remember important chunks of his life, a predicament he blamed on drugs. "I can't remember, for instance, any—*any*—of 1975!" he lamented.

I'M AFRAID WE'RE GOING TO HAVE TO SUBTRACT YOU FROM THE TEAM, NIELS

The Danish physicist Niels Bohr, an excellent athlete in his youth, was the goalkeeper for one of the best soccer teams in Denmark in 1905. Once, while his team was playing a German club, an opposing player launched a long shot toward the Danish goal. Everyone expected Bohr to come out and grab it right away, but instead he stood gawking absentmindedly at one of the goal posts. What was it that had so captured his attention? Some mathematical calculations he had written on the post earlier in the game. The Germans scored, and Bohr never made the national team.

I WAS JUST CHECKING TO SEE IF YOU REMEMBERED

Legendary talent agent and producer Leland Hayward (1902–1971) represented top screenwriters and such high-powered stars as Katharine Hepburn, Gene Kelly, Judy Garland, Fred Astaire,

and Ginger Rogers. One day Rogers complained about a script she had been sent by a certain producer. Hayward went directly to the producer's office. "How can you insult Ginger with such trash, such drivel, such rot!" he shouted. "Get out of here before I throw you out!" the producer yelled back. "You sold us that story!"

LET'S HEAR IT FOR THE POPE

When President Richard Nixon visited the Vatican in 1970, his secretary of defense, Melvin Laird, one of the Vietnam War's chief architects, showed up smoking a huge cigar, which he was promptly told to get rid of before the pope arrived. The secretary of defense obliged, putting it in his pocket—but had neglected to put it out first. Just as the pope appeared, Laird's jacket started to smoke and then caught fire. Laird frantically slapped at his pocket, prompting several other guests to join in what they mistook to be a round of applause for the pontiff.

AND ASKED SOMEONE
WHO WON THE THE CIVIL WAR

American actor Joseph Jefferson (1829–1905) was in the elevator of the New York Stock Exchange building when a man with a familiar face got in. He greeted Jefferson very warmly and graciously, but Jefferson couldn't place the man for the life of him. "I asked him as a sort of feeler how he happened to be in New York," Jefferson explained later to a friend, "and he answered, with a touch of surprise, that he had lived there for several years. Finally, I told him in an apologetic way that I couldn't recall his name. He looked at me for a moment and then he said very quietly that his name was Ulysses S. Grant." The friend asked Jefferson what happened next. "Why, I got out at the next floor."

SIR BENJAMIN,
YOU LOOK SO FLUSHED!

The eminent British surgeon Sir Benjamin Collins Brodie (1783–1862) was deeply engrossed in writing a paper when he was dragged away, against his will, to a formal party. After drinking with some friends for a while, he went into the men's room and prepared to make his escape. He planned to tuck his hat under his arm and sneak past a group of arriving guests. As he crept out, however, the men all started laughing and the women, embarrassed, turned their heads away. In the hall, the perplexed doctor was intercepted by his host, who exclaimed, "Good Lord, Brodie, is that a usual part of your attire?" Brodie turned to look at himself in the hall mirror and saw that instead of his hat, he had picked up the toilet-seat cover.

YOU COULDN'T TELL ONE MOUNTAIN FROM ANOTHER, EITHER

Even animals can have senior moments. Bruno, a St. Bernard rescue dog in the Alps, was famous for forgetting where he was and where he was going. Once, in 1980, a search party had to be sent out to find him, which took more time than recovering the climbers he was supposed to rescue in the first place. That was the eighth time in two years that Bruno had suffered a severe memory lapse, and it brought his employment to an inglorious end.

WHO SAID WE READ BOOKS? WE JUST PUBLISH THEM

An industrywide senior moment occurred in 1975 when Chuck Ross, a writer with a wicked sense of humor, copied in manuscript form the first 20 pages of the 1969 National Book Award–winning novel *Steps*, by Jerzy Kosinski. Ross then submitted it as a sample chapter under his own name and sent it to four publishing houses, including Houghton Mifflin, Kosinski's publisher at the time. They all rejected it. Not satisfied that he had fully made his point, in 1978 and 1979 he sent the entire manuscript of *Steps* to 14 publishers and 13 literary agents. They all rejected it—including Random House, which was the book's original publisher—with no indication that any of them remembered it.

WE'LL JUST BLAME IT ON THE MARTIANS

In 1999 NASA scientists sent the Mars Climate Orbiter 416 million miles to orbit the red planet and study its surface. Two teams were responsible for navigation. Unfortunately, one used American measurements, the other used the metric system, and both forgot to check the other's calculations. Before the spacecraft could make it into orbit, it headed straight down to the planet's surface and crashed.

THE UNIVERSAL GRAVITATION
OF FORGETFULNESS

The scientific genius of Sir Isaac Newton is unquestionable. Not so his memory. One day Dr. William Stukely, a scholar best known for his studies of Stonehenge and a stranger to Newton, called at Newton's house and was told by a servant that Sir Isaac was in his study and couldn't be disturbed. Stukely sat down to wait. A short time later another servant brought in Newton's dinner, a boiled chicken under a cover, and put the dish down on a table next to the visitor. When an hour had passed and Newton still hadn't appeared, the hungry Stukely ate the chicken without thinking. Finally Newton came in and apologized for having kept his visitor waiting. "Give me but leave to take my short dinner," he said, "and I shall be at your service; I am fatigued and faint." Upon removing the cover, he found only a pile of bones. Embarrassed by what he took to be yet another of his frequent lapses of memory, he put back the cover and said, "If it weren't for the proof before my eyes, I could have sworn I hadn't dined."

WE REALLY ARE GOING TO HAVE TO KEEP BETTER TRACK OF OUR POSSESSIONS

In 1986 the National Park Service had an expensive senior moment when it spent $230,000 to buy a parcel of land in Washington, D.C. It was revealed two years later that the Park Service had already bought the land—in 1914.

BLIND JUSTICE

In 1982 a gunman tried to rob a Louisiana motel. He brought along a plastic trash bag in order to mask his identity, but forgot to make holes for his eyes. Once the bag was over his head, he clawed at the plastic while stumbling around the motel lobby, until he was arrested.

HOOPS!

On May 6, 1984, the Dallas Mavericks were playing the Los Angeles Lakers in game four of the National Basketball Association Western Conference semifinals. There were just six seconds left, and Dallas rookie Derek Harper pulled down the rebound of a Laker shot and began to dribble to run out the clock. It's the right strategy when your team's ahead, but unfortunately, the score was tied, a fact that somehow escaped Harper. Neither his incredulous teammates' shouting nor 20,000 Mavericks fans' screaming prevented him from dribbling until the buzzer sounded. The game went into overtime, the Lakers won, they won the next game, too, and went on to the finals. Dallas—and Harper—stayed home.

BUT WE DO HAVE SOME STEAK AND KIDNEY PIES WE CAN THROW AT THEM

The army of British general James Abercromby outnumbered French forces five to one when it attacked at Ticonderoga in New York in 1750. But when Abercromby sent his troops against the French precisely where the enemy's position was strongest, he threw away his advantage. Worse, when the general's gallant but badly depleted army finally reached the nine-foot-tall French fortifications, the assault had to be abandoned because the British had forgotten to bring along ladders to scale them.

NOW, *PROMISE* ME YOU'LL CALL BACK

Michael Robinson won the 1992 British *Sunday Express* Silver Medal for Dubious Distinction when he called the police to deliver a bomb hoax, and then was so worried about the cost of the call that he gave the police his phone number and asked them to call him back.

REMIND ME AGAIN
ABOUT BANKERS' HOURS

When four masked men attempted to rob a bank near Rome in 1980, they forgot to check the closing time and arrived three minutes after the plate-glass entrance door was locked. The leader of the gang tried to break in by throwing himself against the door and was knocked unconscious. His accomplices had to carry him to the get-away car and beat a hasty retreat.

YOU CAN NEVER CATCH A CAB
WHEN YOU NEED TO

When thinking about scientific problems, André-Marie Ampère, the absentminded French physicist, often took a piece of chalk from his pocket and wrote on the nearest convenient surface. Once, while walking in Paris, he was struck with a sudden insight about a particular problem. Seizing the moment, he began to write a series of notes and equations on the first available surface he could find—which happened to be the back of a hansom cab that was parked on the street. When the entire surface was covered, he was shocked to see his "blackboard" pull away and vanish down the street, taking with it the solution to the problem.

I *THOUGHT* MY STEED WAS GOING A LITTLE SLOWER THAN USUAL

When Reverend William Lisle Bowles (1762–1850) took his daily horseback ride on a toll road, he paid the gatekeeper two pence for the privilege. One day Bowles passed alone through the gate on foot, but handed the two pence to the gatekeeper anyway. The man asked him what the money was for. "For my horse, of course," replied Bowles. "But, sir, you have no horse!" exclaimed the gatekeeper. "Oh, am I walking?" asked Bowles, looking around in confusion.

THE STUNT GUYS
MUST HAVE BEEN DEMOCRATS

In 2003, while filming a chase scene, Arnold Schwarzenegger was the victim of a stunt crew's collective senior moment on the set of *Terminator 3*. A member of the crew told him that the first obstacle he'd encounter was a breakaway wall: "You'll crash right through it, no problem." "Okay," said Schwarzenegger, "let's do it." But when filming began, Arnold hit the wall hard, injuring himself. The crew had forgotten to take out a structural beam.

THE FINE POINTS OF
SENIOR MOMENT ETIQUETTE

The British writer and actor Hesketh Pearson was in a London theater one day, waiting to speak to Sir Herbert Beerbohm Tree (1853–1917), an actor himself and the manager of the theater. A few seats away another man was waiting for Tree as well. When Tree finally arrived, he sat down between them and said to both,

"Consider yourselves introduced. I only remember one of your names, and that wouldn't be fair to the other."

THE JOHNSON TOUCH

In 1961 *New York Times* reporter Russell Baker was coming out of the Senate when he ran into Vice President Lyndon Johnson, who grabbed him. "You! I've been looking for you!" LBJ said, and pulled the journalist into his office. He then harangued Baker about how important Baker was to the Kennedy administration and what an insider he was. While he was talking, LBJ scribbled something on a piece of paper, called in his secretary, and handed it to her. She took it, left the room, returned a short time later, and handed the paper back to LBJ, who glanced at it, tossed it away, and then finished his monologue. Baker later learned that Johnson had written: "Who is this I'm talking to?"

AT LEAST IT WASN'T
ANOTHER TECHNICIAN

In the early days of the space program, technicians who had the essential task of cleaning a rocket's fuel tanks before a test flight suffered an embarrassing low-tech senior moment. Since even a speck of dirt could change a rocket's flight pattern with catastrophic results, the technicians climbed into the fuel tank before each launch and cleaned every square inch. But this time, when they climbed out, the instruments monitoring the tank indicated there was still some contamination. There was nothing to do but start all over again, so they opened the hatch of the tank and began to climb down. That's when they realized they had left the ladder inside.

IPSO FACTO, INCORRECTO

The 19th-century scientist, engineer, and professor Osborne Reynolds of the University of Manchester sometimes forgot he was scheduled to give a lecture. Once, after ten minutes had passed, his students, all-too-familiar with his absentmindedness, sent the janitor to fetch him. A few minutes later, Reynolds came tearing into the classroom, pulling on his gown. He took a textbook from the table, opened it at random, and seized upon one formula or another. He wrote the formula on the blackboard and announced it was wrong and that he would now prove his conclusion. Forgetting his students were there, he began mumbling to himself, until finally, without remembering to write down any proof at all, he triumphantly rubbed out the equation and exclaimed that it was, indeed, clearly incorrect.

IN THAT CASE, I'D BETTER START LEARNING MY LINES

When it was becoming obvious that the actor A. E. Mathews (1869–1960) was having trouble learning his lines in a play, he reassured the director: "I know you think I'm not going to learn my lines, but I promise you that even if we had to open next Monday, I would be all right." "But Matty," the director said anxiously, "we *do* open next Monday."

OTHERWISE HE'D BE WRITING A SONATA IN G MAJOR FOR ONE-AND-A-HALF HANDS

Like many absentminded people, Wolfgang Amadeus Mozart often forgot names and places. But his most impressive senior moments came at the dinner table, where his wife cut his meat for him so that he wouldn't forget what he was doing and cut his fingers.

A WATCH POT DOES, IN FACT, BOIL

Sir Isaac Newton's maid once found the great man in the kitchen, standing in front of a pot of boiling water. Baffled, he gazed first at the pot, which contained his watch, and next at his hand, which held an egg.

SEE HOW HIGH MY WITHHOLDING TAX IS? NO WONDER I ROB BANKS!

In 1987, when Kevin Thompson robbed the Mid-Atlantic National Bank in Bloomfield, New Jersey, he forgot his holdup note. So he rewrote it on the back of his paycheck stub, then handed it to a teller, who later handed it over to the police, who now had all the information they needed to find him.

I'D LOVE TO INTRODUCE YOU
TO THE NEW MATHEMATICS FELLOW

When Dr. William Archibald Spooner, the famously absentminded academic administrator and lecturer at Oxford University, invited a faculty member to a tea party "to welcome our new Mathematics Fellow," the man replied, "But, sir, I *am* your new Mathematics Fellow." "Never mind," Spooner said, "come all the same."

AND IT'S IRON LIEGE,
BY A SENIOR MOMENT!

Jockey Willie Shoemaker would have won the 1957 Kentucky Derby but for a world-class senior moment. Coming around the final turn, his horse, Gallant Man, was in the lead and no doubt would have stayed there if the veteran jockey, who had been in hundreds of races, had not forgotten where he was on the track. He mistook the 16th pole, the last one before the finish line, for the finish line itself and stood up in the stirrups in triumph. The horse behind him, Iron Liege, passed him and won the Derby. Shoemaker, one of the greatest jockeys of all time, was suspended for 15 days for his inexplicable memory lapse.

HOW ODD—I THOUGHT
HE WAS STILL A LITTLE BOY

British Prime Minister Lord Salisbury (1830–1903) sometimes forgot what he was wearing. He was once denied admission to a Monte Carlo casino because it had slipped his mind to change out of his dusty walking clothes. At one point he wore a woolen glove on the top of his head to protect himself from drafts and forgot to take it off. It was said that Salisbury was standing behind the throne of Queen Victoria one day when he saw a young man smiling at him. When he asked a friend who the young man was, the astonished reply was, "He's your eldest son."

THAT'S ALL RIGHT, WE DON'T LIKE TRAIN TRAVEL ANYWAY

British author and journalist Lady Georgina Coleridge's great-aunt, Christina, was so absentminded she once tipped a taxi driver with a train ticket to Scotland. According to Lady Georgina, at the end of World War I, when Christina's son John was ordered to travel to southern France to recover from his war wounds, Christina insisted on accompanying him. John had gotten just a few minutes of sleep on their train before it screeched to a halt. It seems Christina had hung her umbrella on the emergency cord, pulling it down as she did so. (Pulling the cord in a non-emergency was, of course, strictly forbidden.) After John apologized profusely for his mother, he went back to sleep, but she prodded him awake after a half hour to tell him how upset she still was that everyone had made such a fuss over her umbrella, when all she had done was hang it up. Which she absentmindedly proceeded to do once more, pulling the cord again. This time they were thrown off the train.

HOW WELL HE FORGETS!

Once, while on vacation, conductor Artur Rodzinski, the director of the New York Philharmonic from 1943 to 1947, was listening to the radio when he tuned into an open-air concert shortly after it began. Fabien Sevitzky was going to conduct Shostakovich's Fifth Symphony, a specialty of Rodzinski's. As Rodzinski listened with increasing appreciation, he turned to those who were with him and marveled, "How well he sustains that line! What excellent balance!" He admitted that he had clearly underestimated Sevitzky's skill. But when the symphony ended, there was no applause, as expected, only the announcer's explanation that the outdoor concert had been rained out and, instead, the station had played a recording of the symphony—conducted by Artur Rodzinski.

DON'T GET ME
TO THE CHURCH ON TIME

When the 18th-century vicar George Harvest had dinner at his friends' homes, he had a habit of saying good-bye at the end of the evening and then, instead of going out the door, heading up his hosts' stairs. He was often discovered sleeping in the wrong house. Most impressive of all, he left the same woman waiting at the altar twice. She was the daughter of the bishop of London, which may explain why the absentminded Harvest was posted to the village of Thames Ditton for the rest of his life.

DID YOU NOTICE HOW SHABBY
HIS HOUSE WAS?

At the University of Königsberg, where mathematician David Hilbert taught in the late 19th century, it was a tradition for each new member of the faculty to make a formal call on the senior professors. When one new colleague called on Hilbert and his wife, the younger man sat down, put his top hat on the floor, and politely started a conversation. However, Hilbert's mind was clearly elsewhere. After a while he picked up the other man's hat, put it on his head, and led his wife out of their own house, saying to her, "My dear, I think we have delayed our good colleague enough."

AND WE BROUGHT BANDAGES, TOO!

In 1960 the young Judi Dench was playing Shakespeare's Juliet at the Old Vic Theatre in London. As she tells it, she was crouching over the lifeless body of her cousin Tybalt, crying out, "Where are my father and my mother, nurse?" when her actual father, a doctor, who was in the audience with her mother and apparently seized by a senior moment, stood up and announced, "Here we are, darling, in row H!"

THIS IS GOING TO HURT MY PRACTICE

A Greek physician named Aesclepiades, who practiced in Rome, was so sure of his medical skill that he swore he would stop being a physician if he ever became ill himself. His boast was never truly tested, however, because while still in good health he absentmindedly fell down a stairway and broke his neck.

I DO ALL MY BEST THINKING IN FLANNEL

Early one Sunday morning the great 18th-century thinker Adam Smith wandered into his garden and began to ponder a deep philosophical question. Without paying any attention to where he was going, he opened his gate and began to walk along the street. He was brought to his senses only by the sound of church bells. People arriving for morning services were astonished by the sight of the eminent philosopher and economist wearing only his nightgown—twelve miles away from his home.

ALTHOUGH THE ONES
I'M USED TO PLAYING FOR
AREN'T USUALLY SO ALERT LOOKING

Walking with a friend one day in New York, Fritz Kreisler (1875–1962), the Vienna-born violinist and composer, passed a large fish shop. Kreisler suddenly stopped, looked at the fish, and snapped out of a senior moment. "Heavens!" he exclaimed to his friend. "That reminds me. I should be playing at a concert!" The fish, arranged in rows, mouths open and eyes staring, had reminded him of a concert audience.

CERTAINLY NOT LIKE
THOSE HEATHENS

In the early 1950s, during a debate on the Middle East problem, Warren Austin, an American diplomat and U.S. delegate to the United Nations, sternly advised Jews and Arabs to "sit down and settle their differences like Christians."

MY LECTURE TONIGHT IS TITLED "YOU WILL ALL BURN IN HELL FOR ETERNITY"

In 1956, when Lord Carrington was the United Kingdom high commissioner in Australia, he visited a small town in the western part of the country. Walking down the aisle of Town Hall to give a speech, Carrington was surprised when, at a signal from the mayor, the entire audience stood up and began to belt out the rousing song "Hold the Fort," based on an incident from the American Civil War. It must have seemed to Carrington that the entire town had suffered a senior moment in its choice of a song, for just as he was about to reach the stage, the voices of the audience rang out: "See the mighty host advancing, Satan leading on! Mighty ones around us falling, courage almost gone!"

THE OSCAR FOR BEST UPSIDE DOWN PICTURE GOES TO . . .

It was the 1947 Academy Awards, and actor Ronald Reagan was presenting the nominees for best picture of the year. As he read from his cue cards, he was supposed to turn around every now and then to make sure that his script was in sync with the film clips being shown behind him. But in an embarrassing senior moment, he forgot to look. If he had, he would have seen that the footage was being shown backward, upside down, and on the ceiling.

WELL, IF THE SHOE FITS . . .

The absentminded Russian composer Alexander Scriabin (1872–1915) once arrived at a party wearing a pair of brand-new boots. But when he returned home, he was wearing a pair of old boots instead, although he couldn't remember putting them on. More astonishingly, the boots didn't even match.

SHOULD YOU NEED
ANOTHER OPERATION,
DON'T HESITATE TO COME BACK

Two Norwegian doctors writing in a 1974 issue of the *Canadian Medical Association Journal* described the case of a young, ambitious 19th-century doctor in Norway who was finishing up a year as the assistant of a renowned surgeon. It was the custom then to have little communication with such an important man, even though they had worked side by side. As the young doctor prepared to leave his assistantship, he arranged with the head nurse for a moment to speak to the surgeon. He then thanked the Great Man for the time he had spent in the department and bid him good-bye. The surgeon peered over his glasses and replied, "Thank you. I hope you have fully recovered and are satisfied with the treatment you received."

AND GAVE HIM THE NAME
"WHITE MAN WITH HEAD IN CLOUDS"

Thomas Nuttall (1786–1859), a pioneer botanist, was known almost as much for his absentmindedness as for his brilliant field work along the Missouri River and in the Pacific Northwest. He had a great talent for wandering away from the rest of the group and getting lost, forcing his colleagues to light beacons to help him find his way back to camp. One night he didn't return at all and a search party was sent out. But Nuttall assumed the searchers were Indians and ran away, getting even more lost. His annoyed colleagues pursued him for three days, until he accidentally wandered back into camp. Another time Nuttall got so lost, he wandered around for hours until he could walk no more and lay down in exhaustion. Fortunately a passing Indian took pity on him, brought him three miles to the nearest river, and paddled him home in a canoe.

A GRAVE IS A HORRIBLE THING TO WASTE

An absentminded doctor pronounced a man dead in Pecaya, Venezuela, in 1971, but when the first shovelfuls of earth were being flung into the man's grave, the unconscious victim, who had suffered a nonfatal heart attack, came to, pushed opened the lid of his coffin, and scrambled out of the hole, screaming and cursing. Sadly, his mother-in-law, who was standing by the side of the grave, promptly dropped dead of shock. She was then buried in the grave intended for her son-in-law, after other doctors made sure she was really, really dead.

TENNYSON, ANYONE?

One day, Alfred, Lord Tennyson's father, the Reverend George Clayton Tennyson, went to visit a parishioner. When a servant answered the door and asked who was calling, Tennyson's mind went blank, and he found to his surprise that, for a few moments, at least, he couldn't summon up his own name. Distraught, he started to walk away, until a village tradesman smiled at him and said, "Good day to you, Dr. Tennyson." "By God, my man," Tennyson replied excitedly, "you're right!"

AT LEAST I DIDN'T LEAVE
MY WALLET IN THE BACKSEAT

Even the celebrated cellist Yo-Yo Ma, who has memorized hundreds of musical compositions, has been laid low by senior moments, none more nearly disastrous than when he left his $2.5 million cello in a taxi after a Carnegie Hall concert. When it was recovered, he was asked how he could have forgotten something so precious. "Practice," he replied.

AND YOU MIGHT ADD MY MEMORY TO THAT LIST, TOO

Anglican archbishop Richard Chenevix Trench (1807–86) retired from the see of Dublin and spent his last two years in London. On returning to visit his successor, Lord Plunkett, in Dublin, Trench's memory lapsed and he forgot that he was no longer the host, remarking to his wife during dinner, "I'm afraid, my love, that we must put this cook down among our failures."

I WANTED TO SEE HOW THE AUDIENCE WAS REACTING

When the actor Frank Benson (1858–1939) played the primitive monster Caliban in *The Tempest,* he was suspended by his ankles, swung across the stage, and beat his chest like Tarzan. One night he launched himself from the wings, his body covered in his bestial, half-fish, half-animal makeup, only to realize he was still wearing his eyeglasses.

YOUR NOSE LOOKS
ESPECIALLY UNFAMILIAR

The Reverend William Spooner (1844–1930), the dean of New College at Oxford University and namesake of "spoonerisms," once ran into an old acquaintance. "Good evening, Dr. Spooner," the man said. "I don't suppose you remember me." Spooner looked at him for a moment and replied, "On the contrary, I remember your name perfectly, but I've completely forgotten your face."

WHY, WE COULD USE ONE
JUST LIKE IT IN OUR NEW FILM!

While discussing the score of a new MGM film, Sam Goldwyn, a great admirer of Cole Porter, told everyone working on the production that they needed a song like "Night and Day." Soon thereafter, the studio chief visited the home of one of his associates, where the song was playing on the phonograph. "What tune is that?" asked Goldwyn.

SOMEBODY'S GOING TO PAY
BIG-TIME FOR THIS

We all remember that Popeye's strength came from cans of spinach, which he slurped down throughout the day. It was in the 1890s that the vegetable was first declared a major source of iron, and during World War II, when iron-rich meat was in short supply, spinach became a familiar alternative. As it turns out, its iron-rich reputation rested on a senior moment. German chemists investigating the claim in the 1930s discovered that the original 19th-century researchers had made a tenfold mistake in calculating spinach's iron content by putting a decimal point in the wrong place. Unfortunately, parents didn't get the word, so it stayed on the plates of millions of suffering children, even though, as the science writer Richard Mould put it, "For a source of iron, Popeye would have been better off chewing the cans."

THE FIFTH ANNUAL
G. K. CHESTERTON AWARD
FOR ABSENTMINDEDNESS
GOES TO . . . G. K. CHESTERTON!

On one occasion, writer G. K. Chesterton was heading off to make a speech when he suffered a senior moment sufficient to force him off the train and telegraph his wife: "Am in Market Harborough. Where ought I be?" She wired back: "Home."

AND AMNESIA IS THE LANGUAGE
OF THE ABSENTMINDED

In 1985 writer and radio personality Nigel Rees asked one of his guests on the BBC Radio program *Quote . . . Unquote* the following question: "Who said 'Violence is the repartee of the illiterate?' " The guest, journalist and author Alan Brien, searched his memory. "I don't think I've heard it before," he said. "Modernish? It can't be very old. Bernard Shaw would be too good for it. Perhaps it's Chesterton. Is it?" The quote was from Brien himself.

IF I WASN'T SUPPOSED TO NAP, WHY WAS THE BED THERE?

At a party at the house of German mathematician David Hilbert (1862–1943), his wife noticed that he hadn't put on a clean shirt. She told him to go upstairs and do so immediately, but he never returned. When she went up to get him, she discovered him fast asleep in bed. Judging from appearances, he had taken off his coat, then his tie, and then his shirt, but had forgotten to put on another shirt and had instead taken off his pants and concluded that he was there to take a nap.

IF I KNEW WHO YOU WERE, THAT WOULD INDICATE THAT I HAD REASON TO REMEMBER YOU

When Winston Churchill was asked "Remember me?" by someone who escaped his memory, he would reply, "Why should I?"

FORTUNATELY, THE X-RAY OF THE SCREWDRIVER WAS NEGATIVE

In 1985 in Cannes, doctors were stunned when an X-ray of a man who was having headaches revealed a seven-inch-long screwdriver in his head! What kind of terrible accident could account for such a thing? How could the patient have survived? It was soon discovered, however, that the screwdriver was not in the man's head after all, but in the X-ray machine. A technician had left it there and forgotten all about it.

NOT *YOU*, OF COURSE. I MEAN THAT *OTHER* TERRIBLE WOMAN

When Sir John Gielgud told Elizabeth Taylor that Richard Burton's acting had gone downhill "since he married that terrible woman," he had clearly forgotten that the woman Burton had married in 1964 was Taylor herself.

UH-OH

In 1989 New York wine merchant William Sokolin was entrusted with selling a bottle of Chateau Margaux 1787 that had once belonged to Thomas Jefferson. At auction, where Sokolin set a minimum price of $500,000 on behalf of an anonymous customer, no bidder would meet his price. Afterward, he had the unfortunate idea of taking it along to dinner at the Four Seasons restaurant. As he was getting ready to leave at the end of the evening, an absentminded waiter carrying a coffee tray suffered a physical senior moment. To the horror of everyone nearby, he bumped into the bottle and broke it, spilling the precious contents across the floor. (Although the bottle was insured, it was for less than half of Sokolin's asking price.)

DO AS I SAY, NOT AS I DON'T SAY

One day Benjamin Jowett, the dean of Balliol College at Oxford University, took a long walk with a student. In the beginning of their walk, the undergraduate made various efforts at starting up a conversation, but the absentminded Jowett was lost in his own thoughts. In fact, he didn't speak to the student at all, only occasionally murmuring to himself before lapsing again into silence. Yet at the end of the walk Jowett turned to the hapless student and advised him in no uncertain terms, "You must cultivate the art of conversation. Good morning!"

AND YOUR BUTTOCKS WILL SOON BE DEAD!

American actor Osgood Perkins (1892–1937) was appearing in a play in which he had to stab another actor with a knife, when one day the prop man forgot to put the weapon on the table. Thinking fast to spare both the absentminded prop man and himself from embarrassment, Perkins kicked the actor in the rear. As the other actor fell down, Perkins announced to the audience, "Fortunately, the toe of my boot was poisoned!"

SEE? THIS PROVES MY POINT

Dallas City Council member Roland Tucker was known as a strong advocate of crime prevention in the 1980s. He even researched making it illegal for people to leave their keys in unattended cars. Naturally, he himself soon left his car keys in the ignition, not to mention leaving his research on preventing crime on the seat. The car, with the key and papers inside, was stolen.

THE TENTH CIRCLE
IS FOR THE FORGETFUL

Diplomatic historian Charles S. Tansill of Georgetown University always kept some cash inside a copy of Dante's *Inferno* for those times when a financial senior moment struck. As he explained later, "When I ask myself, 'Where in hell did I put that money?' I know immediately where it is."

AND I MIGHT EVEN REMEMBER
TO PAY THE FARE

Max Schödel, the 19th-century Austrian painter, once hailed a cab in Vienna, and when the driver asked, "Where to?" Schödel thought it over for a while and replied, "Number six," which is all he could remember for the time being. "I'll tell you the street later on," he told the confused driver.

SADLY, THE 10-POUND NOTES
WERE A TRIFLE OVERCOOKED

It was a very busy New Year's Eve at the New House Hotel in Wales, and chef Albert Grabham chose the safest place he could think of to temporarily put the restaurant's cash and charge slips: the oven. Who would look there? Apparently no one—not even Grabham. The next morning, in preparation for New Year's lunch, he lit the oven with the money still inside.

WE JUST FIGURED FOUR PIECES OF PI WERE BETTER THAN 3.14

The mathematical constant pi, represented by the symbol π, is the ratio of the circumference of a circle to its diameter. It's an infinite decimal but is commonly approximated to 3.14 or 3.14159. You can't get through elementary school without learning it in order to solve simple mathematical problems. Nevertheless, in 1897 the members of the General Assembly of Indiana suffered a collective memory lapse when, without explanation, they passed a bill declaring that the value of pi was 4. This would have ensured that mathematical and engineering calculations throughout the state would go terribly wrong, had not sharper memories prevailed.

BUT I'LL TELL YOU ONE THING:
IT READS LIKE A NOVEL WRITTEN BY
SOMEONE STRUNG OUT ON DRUGS

It has long been known that the use of drugs and alcohol makes it harder to remember what happened under the influence. Even so, Sir Walter Scott seems to have experienced an extraordinary memory lapse while he was addicted to laudanum, an opium-based painkiller. In 1819 Scott read the proofs of his just-completed novel, *The Bride of Lammermoor,* and confessed he didn't recognize a single character, incident, or conversation in the entire work.

IT WAS THE "WHATNOT"
THAT REALLY BROKE THE BUDGET

President Dwight D. Eisenhower created the department known as H.E.W. (Health, Education, and Welfare) in 1953, but he couldn't seem to remember what the letters stood for. He kept calling it "Health, Welfare, and Whatnot."

BEETHOVEN'S FILTH

Beethoven often forgot to keep fires going in his room in the dead of winter. He never remembered to have his windows washed or change his shirts unless someone reminded him. Once, a local policeman, convinced that the great composer was a tramp because Beethoven hadn't remembered to put on fresh clothes for days, threw him in jail. Whereas the ill-tempered composer sometimes threw books at his servants, at other times he absentmindedly overpaid them.

THE SIXTH ANNUAL
G. K. CHESTERTON AWARD
FOR ABSENTMINDEDNESS
GOES TO . . . G. K. CHESTERTON!

Chesterton once wrote to a friend: "On rising this morning, I carefully washed my boots in hot water and blackened my face, poured coffee on my sardines, and put my hat on the fire to boil. These activities will give you some idea of my state of mind. . . ."

NEXT TIME, HOW ABOUT WE
JUST TAP HER ANKLE WITH A STICK?

In the 1930s, in the early days of BBC television, Jasmine Bligh was one of the network's first announcers. The floor managers had decided to cue her by activating a small electrical device tied around her ankle. This device was supposed to deliver a barely perceptible jolt so she would know when to start speaking. In what has to be considered one of the more potentially fatal group senior moments in history, the management forgot to test the setup in advance. The first time it was used, the director in the control room called out "Cue, Jasmine," a button was pushed, and Bligh cried out, "AAAAARRGH! And good evening."

WHAT A CHEAPSKATE!

To impress a woman on a date, entertainer Harry Richman (1895–1972) sometimes tipped a waiter fifty dollars after being handed the menu. Once, Richman asked the head waiter at the deluxe Stork Club, "What's the biggest tip you've ever received?" "A hundred dollars," the waiter told him. So Richman gave the man *two* hundred dollars. "Now tell me," Richman asked, "who gave you the hundred?" "You did, Mr. Richman," the waiter replied.

YET SOMEHOW SHE HAS NO TROUBLE READING ROYALTY STATEMENTS

According to the husband of author Anne Rivers Siddons, when she is preparing to begin work on a new book she becomes so preoccupied that she sometimes walks into walls. Once she put a carton of orange juice out their back door and their kitten in the refrigerator.

SENATOR OUT OF CLOSET AT LAST

One day South Dakota senator Larry Pressler, who served from 1979 to 1997, attempted to leave a routine Commerce Committee meeting but absentmindedly confused one door with another, even though he had been in the room countless times—and entered a closet instead. He was so embarrassed that he decided to stay in the closet until his colleagues left the room via the real exit. Apparently it hadn't occurred to Pressler that the other senators had just witnessed his mistake and were waiting outside the closet to greet him when he finally left— making sure his senior moment entered the lore of Congress.

HOME IS WHERE
THE SHORT-TERM MEMORY IS

In the 1980s, 50-year-old Jermund Skogstad was busy moving into his new apartment in Oslo, Norway, and decided to grab some lunch. But when he finished eating at a café some distance away, he reached into his pocket and realized he had forgotten his wallet, which contained not only his money but also his new address—an address he couldn't remember, no matter how hard he tried. In a newspaper article about Skogstad's plight, the Norwegian said he hoped his new landlady would read the story and rescue him from further embarrassment.

OH, YOU MUST WANT
TO SEE MY DAUGHTER,
WHO'S JUST ABOUT YOUR AGE

The great Irish poet and dramatist William Butler Yeats (1865–1939) was already 54 when his daughter, Anne, was born.

Once, when Yeats and Anne got off the bus that stopped in front of their house in Dublin, Yeats absentmindedly turned and, not recognizing her for a moment as she reached the gate, said hazily, "Oh, and who is it you wish to see?"

FIRST LADY OF FORGETFULNESS

While in the White House, John F. Kennedy found a note with the reminder "Department store—$40,000." Immediately recognizing his wife's handwriting, and familiar with Jackie's shop-a-holic ways, he confronted her. "What the hell is this?" he demanded. She looked at the note, thought for a moment, and said, "I don't remember."

HONEY, I'M *STILL* HAPPY
TO GIVE YOU MY AUTOGRAPH

Doris Day was walking down a Beverly Hills street one day when a man stopped her. Assuming he was a fan, Day said hello and started to move on. "Don't you remember me?" the man called after her. "No," the actress replied. "Should I?" "Well, you didn't have *that* many husbands," replied her second husband, saxophonist George Weidler.

IN PRAISE OF THE ABSENTMINDED

Let's hope that William James (1842–1910) had it right. One day the great psychologist and philosopher was walking down a street in Cambridge, Massachusetts, with two Harvard students when one pointed out a white-bearded man who was talking to himself. The student remarked, "Whoever he is, he's the epitome of the absentminded professor." Replied James, "What you really mean is that he is present-minded somewhere else."

AND FINALLY . . .

Mark Twain, as he did so often, has perhaps the final word on senior moments: "When I was younger," he said toward the end of his life, "I could remember anything, whether it had happened or not; but my faculties are decaying now and soon I shall be so I cannot remember any but the things that never happened."

BIBLIOGRAPHICAL NOTE

All the stories in this book are true (so far as anyone can remember). They were adapted from a great many sources, including books, periodicals, and Web sites—too many, in fact, to list here without straining my memory— but I am especially indebted to the following: *2,500 Anecdotes for All Occasions*, edited by Edmund Fuller (Crown Publishers, 1942, 1970); *Absent-minded?* by James Reason and Klara Mycielska (Prentice-Hall, 1982); *American Literary Anecdotes,* by Robert Hendrickson (Facts on File, 1990); *Awful Moments,* by Phillip Norman (Penguin Books, 1986); *Bartlett's Book of Anecdotes,* edited by Clifton Fadiman and André Bernard (Little, Brown & Co., 1985); *The Book of Heroic Failures,* by Stephen Pile (Ballantine, 1986); *British Literary Anecdotes,* by Robert Hendrickson (Facts on File, 1990); *Broadway Anecdotes,* by Peter Hay (Oxford University Press, 1989); *Bumper Crop,* by Bennett Cerf (Garden City Books, 1952); *The Cannibals in the Cafeteria,* by Stephen Pile (Harper & Row, 1988); *The Cassell Dictionary of Anecdotes,* by Nigel Rees (Cassell, 1999); *Congressional Anecdotes,* by Paul F. Boller (Oxford University Press, 1991); *Duh!* by Bob Fenster (Andrews McNeel, 2000); *Dumb, Dumber, Dumbest,* by John J. Kohut and

Roland Sweet (Plume, 1996); *The Dumbest Moments in Business History,* by Adam Horowitz and the editors of Business 2.0, compiled by Mark Athitakis and Mark Lasswell (Portfolio/Penguin Group, 2004); *Eurekas and Euphorias,* by Walter Gratzer (Oxford University Press, 2002); *The Faber Book of Anecdotes,* edited by Clifton Fadiman (Faber, 1985); *Great Government Goofs,* by Leland H. Gregory III (Dell Publishing, 1977); *Great Operatic Disasters,* by Hugh Vickers (St. Martin's Press, 1985); *The Guinness Book of Humorous Anecdotes,* by Nigel Rees (Guinness Publishing, 1994); *Hollywood Anecdotes,* by Peter Hay (Oxford University Press, 1990); *The Little, Brown Book of Anecdotes,* edited by Clifton Fadiman (Little, Brown & Co., 1985); *The Lives of the Great Composers,* by Harold Schonberg (W. W. Norton, 1981, revised edition); *Lords, Ladies, and Gentlemen,* by Clifton Daniel (Arbor House, 1984); *The Mammoth Book of Oddballs and Eccentrics,* by Karl Shaw (Robin Publishing, Carroll & Graf, 2000); *Mathematics: People, Problems, Results,* by Douglas M. Campbell (Wadsworth Publishing, 1984); *Mould's Medical Anecdotes,* by Richard F. Mould (Institute of Physics Publishing, 1996); *Movie Stars Do the Dumbest Things,* by Margaret Moser, Michael Bertin and Bill Crawford (Renaissance Books, 1999); *My Favorite Intermissions,* by Victor

Borge (Dorset Press, 1971); *Public Speaker's Treasure Chest,* by Herbert Prochnow (Harper & Row, 1963); *The Return of Heroic Failures,* by Stephen Pile (Penguin, 1989); *Rock Stars Do the Dumbest Things,* by Margaret Moser and Bill Crawford (Renaissance Books, 1998); *The Seven Sins of Memory,* by Daniel L. Schacter (Houghton-Mifflin, 2001); *The Speaker's and Toastmaster's Handbook of Anecdotes,* by Jacob Braude (Prentice-Hall, 1971); *Unusually Stupid Americans,* by Kathryn Petras and Ross Petras (Villard, 2003); *What Were They Thinking?* by Bruce Felton (Globe Pequot, 2003); *The Wit's Thesaurus,* by Lance Davidson (Avon Books, 1994); and Anecdotage.com.

—T.F.

INDEX

PHOTO CREDITS:

AP/ Wide World Photos: 4, 6, 13, 16, 21, 22, 28, 30, 33, 37, 39, 41, 45, 48, 49, 50, 53, 54, 58, 66, 72, 79, 84, 85, 86, 95, 98, 102, 105, 114, 119, 120, 122, 124, 127, 129, 137, 140, 142, 149, 152, 155, 157; **Hulton-Deutsch Collection/Corbis:** 138; **The Granger Collection, New York:** 112, 135.

ATTENTION
"SENIORS" OF ALL AGES!

If you've experienced a senior moment you think is good enough to be published, write it down before you forget what it was, then attach it to this form, and send to us at:

Senior Moments
c/o R. Rosen
Workman Publishing
708 Broadway
New York, New York 10003

Submissions must be typed or otherwise completely legible. If we include your senior moment in any future Workman publication, we will credit you (unless otherwise instructed) and send you a complimentary copy. We reserve the right to edit submissions for grammar and considerations of space.

MY SENIOR MOMENT ENTRY FORM
(please print)

Name: _____

Street Address: _____

City/State/Zip: _____

Phone Number: _____

e-mail: _____

I confirm that the attached account of my "senior moment" is true. I understand that my submission becomes the property of Workman Publishing, which will have the right, without further consideration, to use the account in any book, calendar, publication, media, and promotion.

Signed _____

ABOUT THE AUTHOR

Tom Friedman is a writer, editor, and producer who worked for public television in Boston for nearly 25 years. In 1996 he won a Peabody Award for the science documentary series *Odyssey of Life*. He is also the author of two books about business: *Life and Death on the Corporate Battlefield,* with Paul Solman, and *Up the Ladder*. He lives in Northern California.